My First Crochet Book

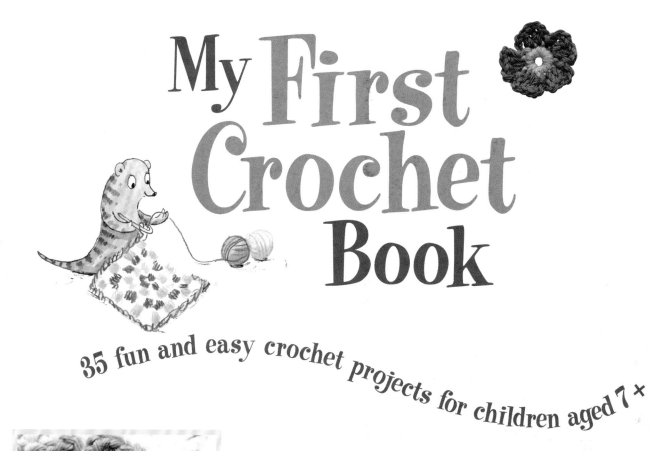

My First Crochet Book

35 fun and easy crochet projects for children aged 7 +

CICO **kidz**

Published in 2013 by CICO Kidz
An imprint of Ryland Peters & Small
519 Broadway, 5th Floor, New York
NY 10012
20–21 Jockey's Fields, London
WC1R 4BW
www.cicobooks.com

10 9 8 7 6 5 4 3 2 1

A CIP catalog record for this book is
available from the Library of
Congress and the British Library.

ISBN: 978-1-908862-94-5

Printed in China

Editor: Katie Hardwicke
Consultants: Marie Clayton, Gillian
Tickle
Designer: Elizabeth Healey
Step artworks: Rachel Boulton
Animal artworks: Hannah George
Photographers: Emma Mitchell and
Martin Norris
For further photography credits, see
page 128.

Contents

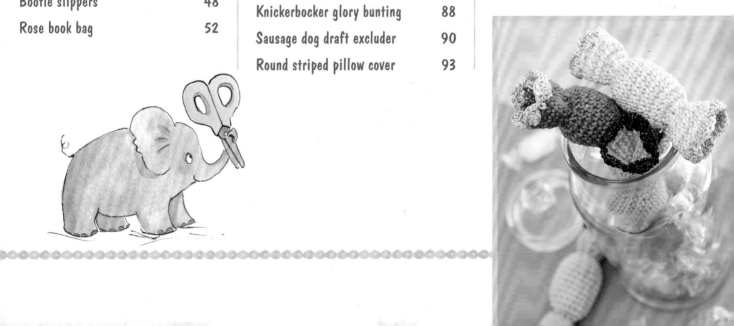

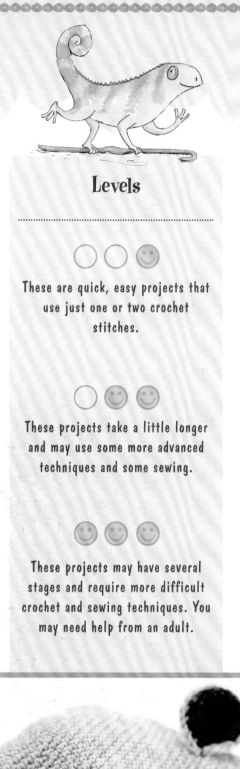

Introduction

These are quick, easy projects that use just one or two crochet stitches.

These projects take a little longer and may use some more advanced techniques and some sewing.

These projects may have several stages and require more difficult crochet and sewing techniques. You may need help from an adult.

Crochet is a great craft that you can quickly learn yourself with just a hook and some yarn. You'll soon be able to make hats, bags, cushions, and cute toys in funky colors, to keep for yourself or to give as gifts. In this book there are four chapters: Clothes and Accessories, with bags, belts, hats, and scarves that will add some fun to your wardrobe; Jewelry, where you'll find a beaded necklace, bracelets, some pretty pins, and even a tiara; Bedroom Essentials, with some fabulous ideas for adding comfortable and colorful pillows and storage ideas to liven up your room; and Perfect Gifts, where you'll find things to make that are ideal presents for your family and all your friends.

Crochet is a great hobby for when you have a quiet moment, perhaps on a long journey, on vacation or on a rainy afternoon. Why not invite a friend over to crochet with you, too? Crochet can be a bit fiddly to learn at the start, but you'll soon master the basic stitches. You can start by learning to make chains, and turn these into friendship bracelets to share. And once you learn to crochet in the round you'll be amazed at how quickly you can create something really impressive, like the cute Mushroom on page 116, or the groovy Round Striped Pillow Cover on page 93.

To help you decide what to make, we have marked all the projects with one, two, or three smiley faces to show how easy or difficult they are. Projects marked with one smiley face are the easiest, two smiley faces mean the project is slightly harder, and those with three smiley faces are the ones to tackle once you've had a bit of practice.

There's a list of all the crochet stitches and techniques you will use at the start of each project, and the pages where you can find the stitch and technique instructions if you need them. There is also a list of everything you will need for each project, including the yarns and colors used in the projects. If you want to, you can choose your own colors and even a different brand of yarn— as long as you use a similar type of yarn (such as worsted or Aran) and the same size hook, the pattern will still work. Some projects need buttons, felt, and scraps of fabric or ribbons, so it's good to put together a sewing box that contains the basics—then you'll be ready to create anything!

Tools and materials

You need just two items to start crocheting: a hook and some yarn. However, there are a few other bits and pieces that you'll need to make some of the projects in this book—but none of them are expensive and you'll probably have some of them at home already.

Crochet hook

Hooks come in different materials and sizes. Each pattern tells you the size you'll need to make the project.

Beads

These are great for adding extra decoration or sparkle to a project. Just sew them on when the crochet is complete or crochet them into the pattern.

Stitch marker

Markers are used, especially in rounds, where you need to keep track of the beginning of a row or a certain point in your crochet. You can use a piece of thread in a bright color or a store-bought marker that looks like a safety pin.

Buttons

Another way of adding color and decoration, buttons are especially good as eyes for toys.

Scissors

Always cut your yarn with scissors, don't break it, even when the pattern says "break yarn."

Sewing needle and thread

You'll need these to sew decorations and felt additions to your projects.

Scraps of fabric

Keep a sewing basket with scraps of fabric, felt, ribbons and trimmings close by you to help finish some of the projects and add your own personal touch.

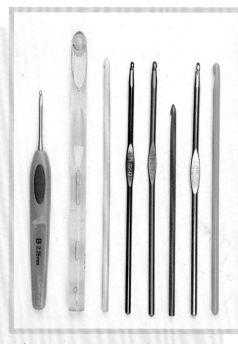

Yarns

You can crochet with all the same yarns that are used for knitting, including some metallic yarns and even string or twine. The projects give you the brand and type of yarn used but if you can't find an exact match you will still be able to crochet using a similar type of yarn. For example, if the pattern uses an Aran weight yarn, any type of Aran yarn can be substituted.

You can find details of the type of yarn on the ball label, together with suggestions for hook sizes.

Crochet techniques

Getting started

Holding the hook
There are two ways of holding the hook in crochet, and you can choose whichever of these feels most natural for you.

Holding the hook like a pen

Holding the hook like a knife

1 Pick up your hook in your right hand if you are right-handed, or left if you are left-handed, as though you were picking up a pen or pencil, or as if you were picking up a knife, if that feels more comfortable.

2 Keeping the hook held loosely between your fingers and thumb, turn your hand so that the palm is facing up and the hook is balanced in your hand and resting in the space between your index finger and your thumb.

Slip knot
The first loop on the hook in crochet is created by a slip knot.

1 Make a loop of the yarn round your fingers, so that the loop is facing downward. Hold the loop at the top, where the yarn crosses, and let the tail drop down so that it falls in the center of the loop. With your free hand or the tip of a crochet hook, pull the tail through the loop so that it makes a second loop (do not pull the end of the yarn all the way through). Pull the knot, so that it tightens loosely.

2 Slip the hook into the second loop and pull the loop taut round the hook. Do not pull it too tightly or the first chain will be hard to make.

Holding the yarn

(1) Pick up the yarn from the ball with your little finger of the opposite hand to your hook, with your palm facing upward—so if you are right-handed pick it up with your left hand, if you are left-handed, pick it up with your right hand.

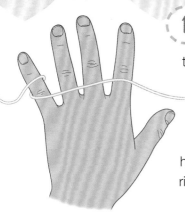

(2) Turn your hand to face downward, with the yarn on top of your index finger and under the other two fingers and wrapped right around the little finger. Hold the hook steady just under the slip knot, then use your left index finger to create tension in the yarn by keeping it held above the work.

Crochet stitches

Yarn over hook

To create a stitch, you'll need to catch the yarn with the hook and pull it through the loop.

(1) Holding the yarn and hook in the appropriate hands, hold the tail end of the yarn under the slip knot and catch the working yarn (the ball end) from behind with the hook pointed upward.

(2) As you gently pull the yarn through the loop on the hook, turn the hook so that it faces downward and slide the yarn through the loop. The loop on the hook should be kept loose enough so that the hook slides through easily.

Chain

Most crochet projects begin with a length of chain. This is the perfect stitch to practice your tension on, as it is the simplest thing you can do in crochet.

(1) Using the hook, wrap the yarn over the hook (see above) and pull it through the loop on the hook, creating a new loop on the hook. One chain is made.

(2) Making sure the stitches are even—not too loose or tight —repeat step 1 to make a length of chain. Keep moving your middle finger and thumb close to the tip of the hook, to hold the work in place with the opposite hand that you hold your hook with.

Slip stitch

A slip stitch doesn't create any height and is often used as the last stitch to create a smooth and even round or row.

1 To make a slip stitch, put the hook through the work, yarn over hook.

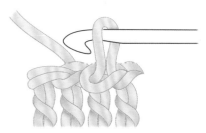

2 Pull the yarn through both the work and through the loop on the hook at the same time. One slip stitch made.

Single crochet (sc)

This is the next crochet stitch to learn once you have got chain right.

1 Make one chain (see page 11). This is called the "turning chain" and you make one at the start of every row of single crochet. Missing the chain you have just made, insert the hook from front to back into the next stitch.

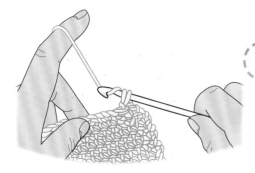

2 There should be the two strands of the stitch and one loop on the hook. Yarn over hook and pull the yarn through the work to the front. Yarn over hook again.

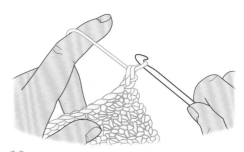

3 Yarn over hook again and pull the yarn through the two loops on the hook. You will then have one loop on the hook. One single crochet made.

Half double crochet (hdc)

This stitch involves a third loop on the hook. You need to work two chain (see page 11) for the turning chain at the start of a row of half double crochet.

 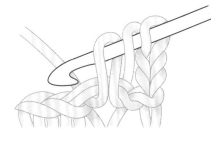 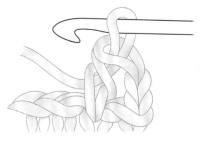

1 Yarn over hook before you insert the hook. Insert the hook in the next stitch, from front to back .

2 Yarn over hook again and pull through the first loop on the hook only (you now have three loops on the hook).

3 Yarn over hook and pull the yarn through all three loops. You'll be left with one loop on the hook. One half-double made.

Double crochet (dc)

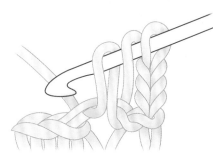 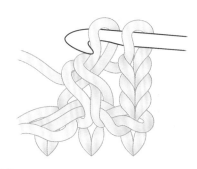 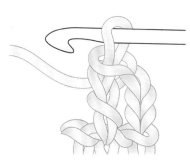

1 Work three chain (see page 11) for the turning chain at the start of a row of double crochet. Before inserting the hook into the work, wrap the yarn over the hook and insert the hook through the work with the yarn wrapped round.

2 Yarn over hook again and pull through the first loop on the hook (you now have three loops on the hook). Yarn over hook again, pull the yarn through two loops (you now have two loops on the hook).

3 Yarn over hook and pull the yarn through the two loops. You will be left with one loop on the hook. One double crochet made.

Treble (tr)

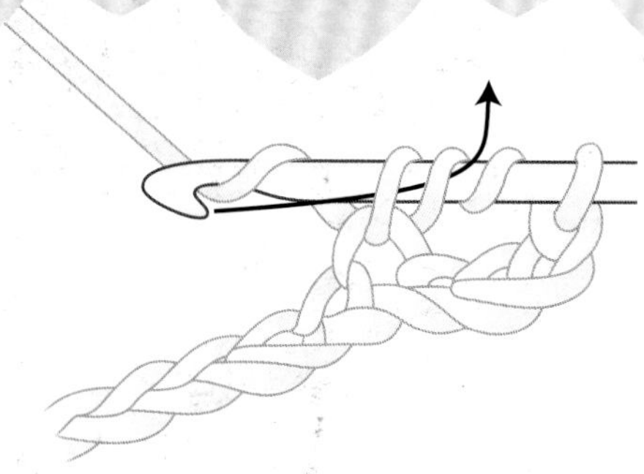

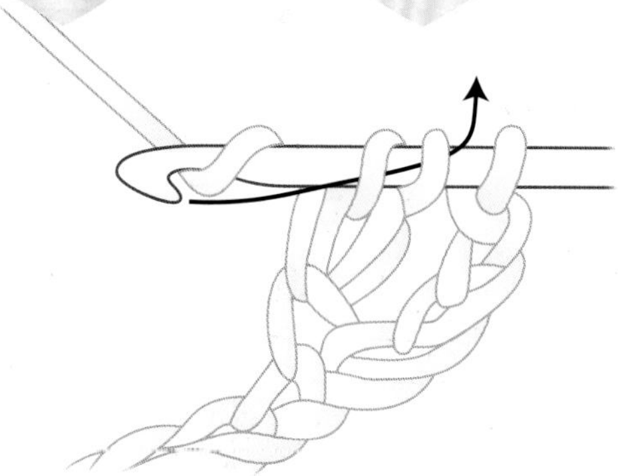

1 Work four chain for the turning chain. Take the yarn over the hook twice, insert the hook into the fifth chain from the hook, yarn over hook, pull a loop through (you now have four loops on the hook). Yarn over hook, pull the yarn through the first two stitches on the hook.

2 There are now three loops on hook. Yarn over hook again, pull a loop through the next two stitches.

3 There are now two loops on hook. Yarn over hook, pull a loop through the last two stitches. You will be left with one loop on the hook. One treble made.

Double treble (dtr)

Work five chain for the turning chain. Yarn over hook three times, insert hook into the stitch, yarn over hook, pull a loop through (five loops on hook), yarn over hook, pull the yarn through two stitches (four loops on hook), yarn over hook, pull a loop through the next two stitches (three loops on hook), yarn over hook, pull a loop through the next two stitches (two loops on hook), yarn over hook, pull a loop through the last two stitches. One double treble made.

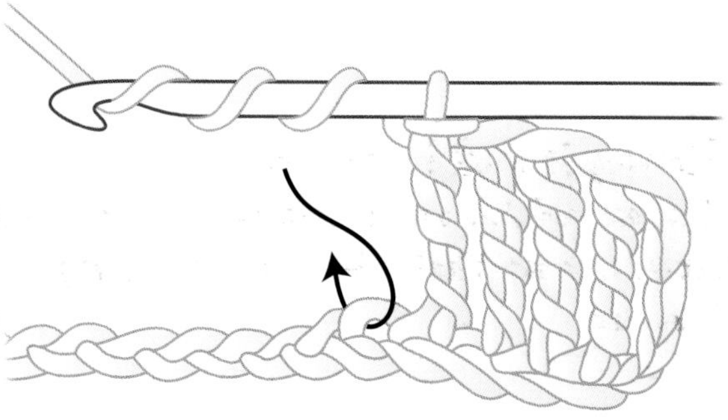

Increasing

To work an extra stitch, you simply need to work into the same stitch more than once. Make two or three stitches into one stitch from the previous row.

The illustration shows a two-stitch increase being made.

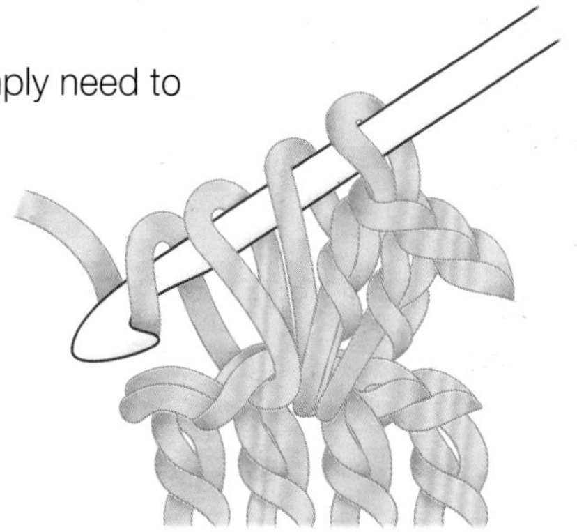

Decreasing

You can decrease by either skipping the next stitch and continuing to crochet, or by crocheting two or more stitches together.

Single crochet two stitches together (sc2tog)

1 Insert the hook into the next stitch, yarn over hook, draw a loop through the stitch, but do not finish the single crochet stitch as usual.

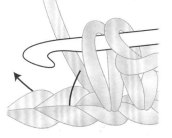

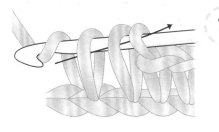

2 Insert the hook in to the next stitch, yarn over hook. Draw the loop through the stitch only (there should be three loops on the hook). Yarn over hook and pull through all three loops on the hook.

Half double two stitches together (hdc2tog)

Yarn over hook, insert hook into next st, yarn over hook, draw a loop through, insert hook into next st, draw a loop through, yarn over hook and pull through all four loops.

Starting to work in the round

If you are crocheting a round shape, one way of starting off is by crocheting a number of chains following the instructions in your pattern, and then joining them into a ring.

1 Work a chain to the length given in the pattern. To join the chain into a circle, insert the crochet hook into the first chain that you made (not into the slip knot)—this creates a horseshoe shape. Yarn over hook, then pull the yarn through the chain and through the loop on your hook at the same time, creating a slip stitch and forming a ring.

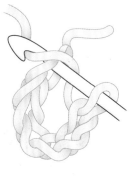

2 You now have a ring. You can either work a continuous spiral (without making a turning chain at the start or joining with a slip stitch at the end), or in complete rounds (see Making fabric on page 16).

Marking rounds with a stitch marker

When rounds are worked in a spiral you do not need to make chain at the start or join the end with a slip stitch, but you will need to know where the round begins and ends.

1 To help you keep your place, mark the beginning of the round with a stitch marker—a piece of yarn in a contrasting color is useful for this or use a store-bought marker. Loop the stitch marker into the first stitch.

2 When you have made a full spiral round and reached the stitch marker, work this stitch, take out the stitch marker from the previous round and put it back into the first stitch of the new round.

Other useful techniques

Turn

This is used when working in rows. Keep the last loop on your crochet hook and turn your work toward you so that it is positioned under your yarn hand. You can then work back down the row on the opposite side.

Making fabric

When making rows or complete rounds you need to make a turning chain at the start or end of the row or round to create the height you need for the stitch you are working. The number of chain needed for each stitch is as follows:
Single crochet – 1 chain
Half double crochet - 2 chain
Double crochet – 3 chain
Treble – 4 chain
Double treble – 5 chain

Working even

Work 1 round or row even means to work the next round without increasing or decreasing any stitches.

Working into back loop (blo)

Insert the hook into the back loop of the next stitch only.

Working into front loop (tfl)

Insert the hook into the front of the next stitch only.

Working into a chain space

Insert the hook into the space between stitches in the row below instead of into the top of the stitch.

Fastening off

When you have finished crocheting, you need to fasten off the stitches to stop all your work raveling.

Pull up the final loop of the last stitch to make it bigger. Cut the yarn, leaving a tail of approx 4 in. 10 cm). Pull the tail all the way through the loop and pull the loop up tightly.

Joining in new yarn

Sometimes you will need to change yarn color, but it's very easy to do.

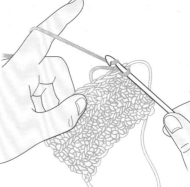

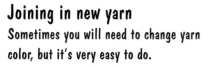

1 Fasten off the old color (see above). Make a slip knot with the new color (see page 10). Insert the hook into the stitch at the beginning of the next row, then insert the hook through the slip knot.

2 Pull the loop of the slip knot through to the front of the work. Yarn over hook with the new color. Work one chain (see page 11) to hold the new color in place, then complete the first stitch as normal.

Weaving in yarn ends

It is important to finish your crochet correctly and weave in the tail ends of the yarn so that they are secure and your crochet won't ravel. Thread a darning needle with the tail end of yarn. On the wrong side, take the needle through the crochet one stitch down on the edge, then take it through the stitches, working in a gentle zigzag. Work through 4 or 5 stitches then return in the opposite direction. Remove the needle, pull the crochet gently to stretch it, and trim the end.

Sewing up

Sewing up crochet fabric can be done in many ways, but using a whip stitch is the easiest. However, you will be able to see the stitches clearly so you can make a feature of them by using a different color yarn to the one used in the project.

Lay the two pieces to be joined next to each other with right sides facing upward. Secure the yarn to one piece. Insert the needle into the front of one piece of fabric, then up from the back of the adjoining fabric. Repeat along the seam.

Sewing on buttons

You can use buttons as decorations—and you never know when you'll need to sew a button onto a piece of clothing!

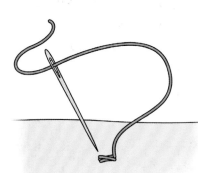

1 Mark the place where you want the button to go. Push the needle up from the back of the fabric and sew a few stitches round and round in this place.

2 Now bring the needle up through one of the holes in the button. Push the needle back down through the second hole and through the fabric. Bring it back up through the first hole. Repeat this five or six times. If there are four holes in the button, use all four of them to make a cross pattern. Make sure that you keep the stitches close together under the middle of the button.

3 Finish with a few small stitches round and round on the back of the fabric and then trim the thread.

Following crochet patterns

To make the projects in this book, you will need to follow the patterns. These give instructions on how many and what type of stitches you need. Crochet patterns use abbreviations for the stitches, such as ch for chain and sc for single crochet. Patterns combine different numbers of stitches and, sometimes, different types of stitches, to make the shape of the crocheted piece.

Crochet patterns are written out as instructions, one row or round at a time. Start by making the number of chain required and then work each row. To help you to keep track of where you are, tick off each row with a pencil when you have completed it.

Sometimes the pattern will include the number of stitches that you should have at the end of each row, shown in brackets. Check that your stitch number matches.

First, practice the basic stitches, how to join in new colors and fasten off, by making a few rectangles or circles. Once you feel happy that you can work all the different types of stitches, you will be ready to start on your very own project.

Finishing your project will involve some different techniques, from sewing up the pieces to sewing on buttons, or attaching pompoms. You'll find instructions on how to do this with each project.

Abbreviations

The following abbreviations are used in the crochet patterns.

beg beginning

blo back loop only

ch chain

ch sp chain space

cont continue

cm centimeters

dc double crochet

dc2tog double crochet 2 together

htr half treble crochet

htr2tog half treble 2 together

in inches

rem remain(ing)

rep repeat

rnd round

sc single crochet

sl st slip stitch

st(s) stitch(es)

sp space

tfl through front loop

tr treble

dtr double treble

CHAPTER 1

Clothes and Accessories

Belt

An extremely simple belt, which can easily be made longer,
or shorter, or wider, as you wish.

You will need

1 x 1¾ oz (50 g) ball (137 yd/125 m)
Debbie Bliss Ecobaby (100%
organic cotton), in each of:

Yarn A: shade 04, aqua

Yarn B: shade 14, lemon

Yarn C: shade 23, peach

Yarn D: shade 24, salmon

D/3 (3.25 mm) crochet hook

Two very small buttons, approx.
½ in. (1 cm) diameter

Sewing needle and thread

Measurements

One size, 1 in. (2.5 cm) wide and
36 in. (92 cm) long

Gauge

Approx. 20 sts and 13.5 rows to
4 in. (10 cm) in hdc using D/3
(3.25 mm) hook, or size required to
obtain correct gauge.

1 Crochet the belt
Using D/3 (3.25 mm) hook and yarn A, ch172.
Row 1: 1hdc in 2nd ch from hook, 1hdc in
each ch to end of row, turn. (170 hdc)
Change to yarn B, fasten off yarn A, and work 1 row
even in hdc, turn.
Change to yarn C, fasten off yarn B, and work 1 row
even in hdc, turn.
Change to yarn D, fasten off yarn C, and work 1 row
even in hdc.
Fasten off yarn.

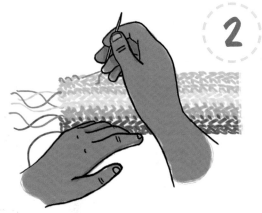

2 Finish the belt
Weave in the loose ends
with a darning needle.

3 Attach the buttons
Sew the buttons to one end of the belt.
To fasten around your waist, insert the
buttons through holes between stitches at
the place where the belt fits you.

Perfect with any outfit!

Abbreviations (see page 19)

ch chain

hdc half double crochet

Techniques (see pages 10–19)

Fastening off

Joining in a new color

Turn

Sewing on buttons

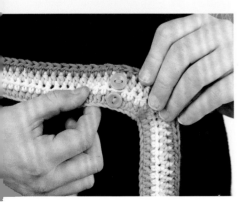

Cowl

A very quick project, worked in the round, so no sewing up! Try using lots of different scraps of yarn for a rainbow-colored neck warmer.

You will need

1 x 3½ oz (100 g) ball (144 yd/132 m) Artesano Aran (50% superfine alpaca, 50% Peruvian highland wool), in each of:

Yarn A: shade 2184, meadle

Yarn B: shade 5083, lomond

H/8 (5 mm) crochet hook

Darning needle

Measurements

One size, approx. 4 in. (10 cm) wide and 47 in. (120 cm) around

Gauge

Approx. 3 grouped double crochets and 7 rows to 4 in. (10 cm) using H/8 (5 mm) hook, or size required to obtain correct gauge.

1 Crochet the cowl

Using H/8 (5 mm) hook and yarn A, ch120, join into a ring with a sl st into first ch, trying not to twist the chain.

Rnd 1: Ch3, 2dc into bottom of same ch, ch1, skip 2 ch, *3dc in next ch, ch1, skip 2 ch; rep from * to end of rnd, join to top of 3-ch with a sl st.

Rnd 2: Sl st in next 1-ch sp, ch3, 2dc in 1-ch sp, ch1, *3dc in next 1-ch sp, ch1; rep from * to end of rnd, join to top of 3-ch with a sl st. Fasten off yarn A.

Rnd 3: Join yarn B to any 1-ch sp with a sl st, ch3, 2dc in 1-ch sp, ch1, *3dc in next 1-ch sp, ch1; rep from * to end of rnd, join to top of 3-ch with a sl st. Fasten off yarn B.

Rnd 4: Join yarn A to any 1-ch sp with a sl st, ch3, 2dc in 1-ch sp, ch1, *3dc in next 1-ch sp, ch1; rep from * to end of rnd, join to top of 3-ch with a sl st. Fasten off yarn A.

Rnd 5: Rep Rnd 3. Fasten off yarn B.

Rnd 6: Join yarn A to any 1-ch sp with a sl st, ch3, 2dc in 1-ch sp, ch1, *3dc in next 1-ch sp, ch1; rep from * to end of rnd, join to top of 3-ch with a sl st.

Rnd 7: Sl st to next 1-ch sp, ch3, 2dc in 1-ch sp, ch1, *3dc in next 1-ch sp, ch1; rep from * to end of rnd, join to top of 3-ch with a sl st. Fasten off yarn.

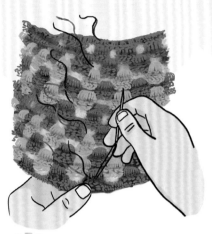

2 Finish the cowl

Use the darning needle to weave in the ends of the yarn.

Abbreviations (see page 19)

ch chain

ch sp chain space

dc double crochet

rep repeat

rnd round

sl st slip stitch

sp space

Techniques (see pages 10–19)

Fastening off

Joining in a new color

Making fabric

Starting to work in the round

NOTE The cowl is worked in complete rounds.

3 Blocking

Ask an adult to help you carefully press the cowl into shape on a soft surface. Use a medium hot iron and put a clean cloth or tea towel over the crochet to protect it from the iron. This is known as blocking.

Flower earmuffs

If you don't like hats, but can't stand having cold ears, earmuffs are for you—and they are also great for when your friends just talk too loudly!

You will need

1 x 1¾ oz (50 g) ball (131 yd/120 m) Rico Essentials Merino DK (100% merino wool), in each of:

Yarn A: shade 19, mulberry

Yarn B: shade 01, rose

Yarn C: shade 04, acacia

US 6 (4 mm) crochet hook

Stitch marker

Darning needle

Fiberfill stuffing

Measurements

One size, approx. 11½ in. (29cm) from center of one earmuff, across strap, to center of other earmuff

Gauge

Approx. 22 sts and 20 rows to 4 in. (10 cm) in sc using US 6 (4 mm) crochet hook, or size required to obtain correct gauge.

1 Crochet the strap

Using US 6 (4 mm) crochet hook and yarn A, ch13.

Row 1: 1sc in 2nd ch from hook, 1sc in each ch to end of row, turn. (12 sc)

Row 2: Ch1, sc in each st across row, turn.

Rep last row until strap is approx. 11 in. (28 cm) long.

Fasten off yarn.

For a matching skinny scarf, simply follow the pattern for the strap and make it longer.

2 Crochet the earpieces (make 4)

Using US 6 (4 mm) crochet hook and yarn A, ch2.

Rnd 1: 6sc in first ch made, do not join rnd.

Rnd 2: 2sc in each sc around. (12 sc)

Rnd 3: [2sc in next st, 1sc] around. (18 sc)

Rnd 4: [2sc in next st, 2sc] around. (24 sc)

Rnd 5: [2sc in next st, 3sc] around. (30 sc)

Rnd 6: [2sc in next st, 4sc] around. (36 sc)

Rnd 7: [2sc in next st, 5sc] around. (42 sc)

Rnd 8: [2sc in next st, 6sc] around. (48 sc)

Rnd 9: [2sc in next st, 7sc] around. (54 sc)

Rnd 10: [2sc in next st, 8sc] around. (60 sc)

Fasten off yarn.

Abbreviations (see page 19)

ch chain

rep repeat

rnd round

sc single crochet

sc2tog single crochet 2 together

sl st slip stitch

Techniques (see pages 10–19)

Fastening off

Joining in a new color

Marking rounds with a stitch marker

Sewing up

Starting to work in the round

Turn

NOTE Earpieces are worked in continuous spiral rounds, do not turn throughout and do not join rounds.

Flowers are worked in complete rounds, joining each round with a sl st.

The strap is worked in rows, turn at the end of each row.

 Crochet the flowers

Using US 6 (4 mm) crochet hook and yarn A, ch6 and join into a ring with a sl st into first ch.

Rnd 1: Ch1, 12sc into ring, join with a sl st into top of 1-ch.
Fasten off yarn A and join in yarn B to any sc.

Rnd 2: 1sc in same st as join [ch5, skip 1sc, 1sc in next st] six times, finishing last rep with a sl st in next st. (6 petals)

Rnd 3: [9sc in next ch sp, sl st in sc] around.
Fasten off yarn B and join yarn A to any sc, work 1 rnd in sc all around petal edges.
Fasten off yarn.

4 Crochet the ties

Using US 6 (4 mm) crochet hook and yarns B and C held together, crochet two lengths of chain, each approx. 20 in. (50 cm) long. When working with two strands, treat them as one, hooking and pulling them through the loops together.

5 Sew the earpieces

Weave in all the loose ends with the darning needle. Take two of the circles that you made for the earpieces and sew them together around the edge, leaving a gap in the edge to stuff them. Fill the earpiece with fiberfill stuffing until it is firm and well-rounded, and then sew up the gap. Repeat with the remaining two circles.

6 Sew on the flowers

Sew a flower to the top of each earpiece, taking a few stitches through the middle with matching yarn. Sew the earpieces to the ends of the strap, with the flowers facing out.

Wrap up warm!

Add the ties

7 Sew one chain to the bottom of each earpiece to make the ties and finish the earmuffs.

Floral purse

This is a really pretty coin purse to make—a great beginner's project, which takes only a small amount of time to achieve maximum effect.

You will need

1 x 1¾ oz (50 g) ball (98 yd/90 m) Debbie Bliss Cashmerino Aran (55% merino wool, 33% microfiber, 12% cashmere) in:

Yarn A: shade 011, green

Small lengths of DK yarn in pinks, purples, blues and yellow for flowers

US 7 (4.5 mm) and US 6 (4 mm) crochet hooks

Darning needle

1 button, ½ in. (1 cm) diameter

Sewing needle and thread

Measurements

Approx. 6 x 4 in. (15 x 10 cm)

Gauge

Exact gauge isn't important for this project.

1 Crochet the purse

Using US 7 (4.5 mm) hook and yarn A, ch24.

Row 1: 1hdc in second ch from hook, 1hdc in each ch to end, 2ch, turn. (22 sts—2ch counts as first hdc).

Row 2: 1hdc in each st, 2ch, turn.

Rep Row 2 until work measures approx. 7½ in. (19 cm).

2 Crochet the flap

Rows 1–4: Ch2, hdc2tog, 1hdc in each st to end, turn. (18 sts)

Rows 5–7: Ch2, hdc2tog, 1hdc in each st to last 2 sts, hdc2tog, turn. (12 sts)

3 Make a buttonhole

Row 1: Ch2, hdc2tog, 1hdc in each of next 2 sts, 2ch, skip 2 sts, 1hdc in each of next 3 sts, hdc2tog, turn.

Row 2: Ch2, hdc2tog, 1hdc in next st, 2hdc in ch sp, 1hdc in each of next 3 sts, turn. (8 sts)

Pretty flowers for a special purse

4 Crochet the edging

Turn and make 32sc sts along first side, 3sc into corner st, 22sc sts along bottom edge, 3sc into corner st, 32sc sts along second side.

Fasten off yarn.

Abbreviations (see page 19)

....

ch chain

ch sp chain space

dc double crochet

hdc half double crochet

hdc2tog half double crochet 2 together

rep repeat

rnd round

sc single crochet

sl st slip stitch

st(s) stitch(es)

Techniques (see pages 10–19)

....

Fastening off

Joining in a new color

Turn

Sewing on buttons

Sewing up

Starting to work in the round

Crochet the flowers (make 4)

5 Use two colors for each flower.
Using first color and US 6 (4 mm) hook, ch6, join into a ring with a sl st into first ch.
Make 16sc into ring, joining tail around into each st, join with a sl st.
Fasten off yarn.
Join second color into fastened-off st.
*Ch3, 1dc in each of next two sts, ch3, sl st in next st; rep from * 4 more times.
(5 petals)
Fasten off yarn.
Pull the yarn tail to close up center hole and sew in the ends.

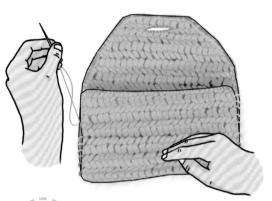

Sew the purse

6 Ask an adult to help you block the purse by pressing it lightly with a warm iron, use a dish towel to protect the yarn if necessary. With the wrong side of the purse facing you, turn up the bottom edge to the start of the flap. Using a darning needle and matching yarn, sew the side seams together with whip stitch, leaving the flap open.

Finish the purse

7 Position the button on the front of the purse to correspond with the buttonhole and sew it in place with a sewing needle. Sew three flowers to the front flap and one to the back of the purse.

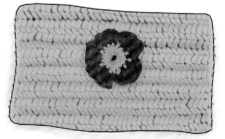

You can use any left-over yarn for the flowers.

Legwarmers

Crochet these cozy legwarmers in one shade or in candy color stripes. They look great with ballet flats or with ankle boots.

You will need

1 x 1¾ oz (50 g) ball (109 yd/100 m) Rico Essentials Soft Merino Aran (100% merino wool), in each of:

Yarn A: shade 041, eucalyptus

Yarn B: shade 015, fuchsia

Yarn C: shade 050, pistachio

US 7 (4.5mm) and H/8 (5 mm) crochet hooks

Darning needle

Measurements

One size, approx. 10¼ in. (26 cm) long and 5½ in. (14 cm) wide, but you can make them longer or shorter by working additional or fewer rounds

Gauge

Approx. 11 sts and 10 rows to 4 in. (10 cm) in pattern using H/8 (5 mm) hook, or size required to obtain correct gauge.

1 Crochet the legwarmers (make 2)

Using US 7 (4.5 mm) hook and yarn A, ch34, join into a ring with a sl st into first ch.

Rnd 1: Ch2, skip next ch, [1sc in next ch, ch1, skip next ch] to end, join with a sl st into top of 2-ch.

Rnd 2: Ch1, 1sc in 1-ch sp, [ch1, 1sc in 1-ch sp] to end, join with a sl st into top of first 1-ch.

Rnd 3: Ch2, [1sc in next 1-ch sp, ch1] to end, join with a sl st into top of 2-ch.

Change to yarn B and larger H/8 (5 mm) hook.

Rnd 4: Ch3, 1dc in each sc and 1-ch sp around, join with a sl st into top of 3-ch. (34 sts)

Change to yarn C and work two rnds even in dc.

**Change to yarn A and work one rnd even in sc.

Change to yarn B and work one rnd even in dc.

Change to yarn C and work two rnds even in dc.**

Rep from ** to ** three times more, or until desired length of legwarmer has been reached.

Change to yarn A and smaller US 7 (4.5 mm) hook.

Next rnd: Ch2, skip next dc [1sc in next dc, ch1, skip next dc] to end, join with a sl st into top of 2-ch.

Next rnd: Ch1, 1sc in 1-ch sp, [ch1, 1sc in 1-ch sp] to end, join with a sl st into top of first 1-ch.

Next rnd: Ch2, [1sc in next 1-ch sp, ch1] to end, join with a sl st into top of 2-ch.

Fasten off yarn.

Keep your ankles cozy

2 Finishing

Use a darning needle to weave in the ends of the different color yarns.

Abbreviations (see page 19)

ch chain

dc double crochet

rep repeat

rnd round

sc single crochet

sl st slip stitch

sp space

st(s) stitch(es)

Techniques (see pages 10–19)

Fastening off

Joining in a new color

Starting to work in the round

Beanie hat

A very cute and simple beanie hat, which will work up in no time at all in the easiest of stitches. You can make it more fun by adding funny animal ears and a face, or just wear it plain and simple!

You will need

1 x 3½ oz (100 g) ball (218 yd/200 m) Rico Essentials Soft Merino Aran (100% merino superwash), in each of:

Yarn A: shade 81, fawn

Yarn B: shade 15, violet (only very small quantities used)

US 7 (4.5 mm) crochet hook

Darning needle

Scraps of white and colored felt for the eyes

Sewing needle and thread

Two buttons for eyes

Left-over pink yarn for nose

Measurements

S(M:L)

Finished hat approx. 19(21:22½) in. [48(52.5:57) cm] unstretched

Gauge

17 sts and 21 rows to 4 in. (10 cm) in sc in the round using a US 7 (4.5 mm) hook, or size required to obtain correct gauge.

1 **Crochet the hat**

Using US 7 (4.5 mm) hook and yarn A, ch2.

Rnd 1: 6sc in first ch, join into a ring with a sl st.

Rnd 2: Ch1, 2sc in each st, join with a sl st into top of 1-ch. (12 sc)

Rnd 3: Ch1, [1sc, 2sc in next st] around, join with sl st into top of 1-ch. (18 sc)

Rnd 4: Ch1, [2sc, 2sc in next st] around, join with a sl st into top of 1-ch. (24 sc)

Rnd 5: Ch1, [3sc, 2sc in next st] around, join with a sl st into top of 1-ch. (30 sc)

Rnd 6: Ch1, [4sc, 2sc in next st] around, join with a sl st into top of 1-ch. (36 sc)

Rnd 7: Ch1, [5sc, 2sc in next st] around, join with a sl st into top of 1-ch. (42 sc)

Rnd 8: Ch1, [6sc, 2sc in next st] around, join with a sl st into top of 1-ch. (48 sc)

Rnd 9: Ch1, [7sc, 2sc in next st] around, join with a sl st into top of 1-ch. (54 sc)

Rnd 10: Ch1, [8sc, 2sc in next st] around, join with a sl st into top of 1-ch. (60 sc)

Work 1 rnd even.

Rnd 12: Ch1, [9sc, 2sc in next st] around, join with a sl st into top of 1-ch. (66 sc)

Work 1 rnd even.

Rnd 14: Ch1, [10sc, 2sc in next st] around, join with a sl st into top of 1-ch. (72 sc)

Work 1 rnd even.

Rnd 16: Ch1, [11sc, 2sc in next st] around, join with a sl st into top of 1-ch. (78 sc)

M and L sizes only

Work 1 rnd even.

Rnd 18: Ch1, [12sc, 2sc in next st] around, join with a sl st into top of 1-ch. (84 sc)

Work 1 rnd even.

Rnd 20: Ch1, [13sc, 2sc in next st] around, join with a sl st into top of 1-ch. (90 sc)

L size only

Work 1 rnd even.

Rnd 22: Ch1, [14sc, 2sc in next st] around, join with a sl st into top of 1-ch. (96 sc)

All sizes

Work even in sc for a further 4¾(5:5½) in. [12(13:14) cm]. Fasten off yarn.

Abbreviations (see page 19)

ch chain

rep repeat

rnd round

sc single crochet

sc2tog single crochet 2 together

sl st slip stitch

st(s) stitch(es)

Techniques (see pages 10–19)

Fastening off

Making fabric

Sewing on buttons

Starting to work in the round

Turn

NOTE The beanie is worked in complete rounds.

The ears are worked in rows, turn at the end of each row.

Try making the beanie in black and white for a very stylish panda version!

2 Crochet the ears (make 2)

Using US 7 (4.5 mm) hook and yarn A, ch2.

Row 1: 4sc in first ch, turn.
Row 2: Ch1, 2sc in each st to end, turn. (8 sc)
Row 3: Ch1, [1sc, 2sc in next st] to end, turn. (12 sc)
Row 4: Ch1, [2sc, 2sc in next st] to end, turn. (16 sc)
Row 5: Ch1, [3sc, 2sc in next st] to end, turn. (20 sc)
Row 6: Ch1, [4sc, 2sc in next st] to end. (24 sc)

Fasten off yarn.

Using US 7 (4.5 mm) hook and yarn B, ch2.
Row 1: 4sc in first ch, turn.
Row 2: Ch1, 2sc in each st to end, turn. (8 sc)
Row 3: Ch1, [1sc, 2sc in next st] to end, turn. (12 sc)
Row 4: Ch1, [2sc, 2sc in next st] to end, turn. (16 sc)
Row 5: Ch1, [3sc, 2sc in next st] to end. (20 sc)

Fasten off yarn.

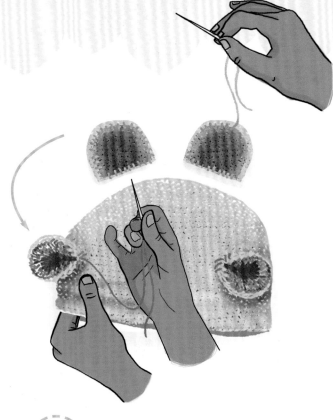

3 Sew the ears

Sew the smaller ear piece onto the larger ear piece. Fold the ear along the straight seam, sew the fold together and then sew the ear to the side of the hat.

4 Sew the eyes

Cut two circles from the white felt and two slightly smaller circles from the colored felt. You can either cut the circles freehand or use something round, such as a large button or cotton reel, to draw around. Sew the white circles to the front of the hat with a sewing needle and thread. Attach the colored circles over the white circles by sewing the buttons on over them.

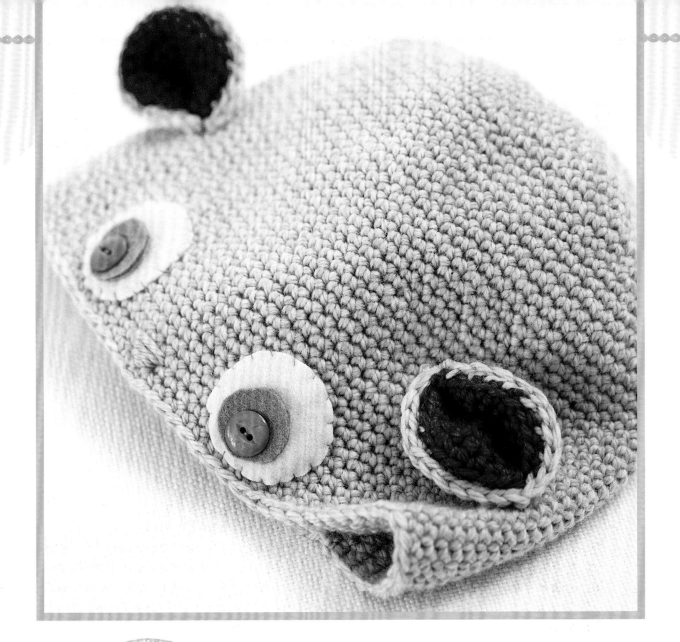

5 Add the nose

Using a scrap of yarn, embroider a triangular nose with a few straight stitches that decrease in size.

Make one for your best friend

Squares scarf

Granny squares are traditional, fun, and easy to make, and once you start on them, you will quickly become hooked! Join lots of squares together to make a lovely, simple scarf.

You will need

....

1 x 1¾ oz (50 g) ball (98 yd/90 m) Patons Fairytale Dreamtime DK (100% pure wool), in each of:

Yarn A: shade 4953, pink

Yarn B: shade 4954, lilac

Yarn C: shade 4957, turquoise

Yarn D: shade 4952, lime

Yarn E: shade 4960, yellow

US 7 (4.5 mm) crochet hook

Darning needle

Measurements

....

One size, approx. 6 x 44 in. (15 x 112 cm)

Gauge

....

Each square measures approx. 3¼ x 3¼ in. (8 x 8 cm) using a US 7 (4.5 mm) hook, or size required to obtain correct gauge.

1 Crochet a square

You can make as many squares as you need, our scarf uses 28. Make an even number if your scarf is going to be two squares wide, like ours.

Using any yarn and US 7 (4.5 mm) hook, ch4, join to first ch with a sl st to form ring.

Rnd 1: Ch3 (counts as first dc), 2dc in ring, ch3, [3dc in ring, ch3] three times, join with a sl st to top of first ch, sl st to next 3-ch sp.

Rnd 2: Ch3 (counts as first dc), [2dc, ch3, 3dc] all in same 3-ch sp, ch1, *[3dc, ch3, 3dc] all in next 3-ch sp, ch 1; rep from * twice more, join with a sl st to top of first ch, sl st to next 3-ch sp.

Rnd 3: Ch3 (counts as first dc), [2dc, ch3, 3dc] all in same sp for corner, ch1, 3dc in next 1-ch sp, ch1, *[3dc, ch3, 3dc] all in next 3-ch sp for corner, ch1, 3dc in next 1-ch sp, ch1; rep from * around, join with a sl st to top of first ch, sl st to next 3-ch sp.

Fasten off yarn.

2 Sew the squares together

Lay your finished squares out in the scarf shape, two squares wide. Move the squares around until you are happy with their positions, if you are using different colors. Using a darning needle and matching yarns, sew all the squares together with whip stitch to make a scarf two squares wide and 14 squares long.

Granny will love your granny squares!

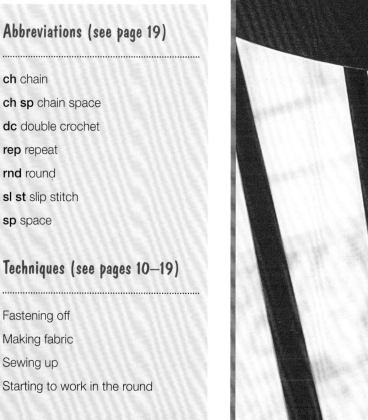

Abbreviations (see page 19)

ch chain

ch sp chain space

dc double crochet

rep repeat

rnd round

sl st slip stitch

sp space

Techniques (see pages 10–19)

Fastening off

Making fabric

Sewing up

Starting to work in the round

Bird bag

A sweet and simple book bag, you can easily make yours into any creature that you wish—ours is a robin redbreast. Try stripes for a tiger!

You will need

1 x 3½ oz (100 g) ball (144 yd/132 m) Artesano Aran (50% superfine alpaca, 50% Peruvian highland wool), in each of:

Yarn A: shade 0042, wester

Yarn B: shade 969, ash

H/8 (5 mm) crochet hook

Darning needle

Felt and buttons for features

Sewing needle and thread

Measurements

One size, approx. 9½ x 9¾ in. (24 x 25 cm)

Gauge

Approx. 14 hdc and 12 rows to 4 in. (10 cm) in hdc using H/8 (5 mm) hook, or size required to obtain correct gauge.

1 Crochet the bag
Using H/8 (5 mm) hook and yarn A, ch72.
Row 1: 1hdc in 3rd ch from hook, 1hdc in each ch to end of row, turn. (70 hdc)
Row 2: Ch2, 1hdc in each st across row, turn.
Work even in hdc as row 2, until work measures approx. 7 in. (18 cm).
Change to yarn B and work a further 2½ in. (6 cm) even in hdc.
Fasten off yarn.

2 Crochet the straps (make 2)
Using H/8 (5 mm) hook and yarn A, ch8.
Row 1: 1hdc in 3rd ch from hook, 1hdc in each ch to end of row, turn. (6 hdc)
Row 2: Ch2, hdc in each st across row, turn.
Work even in hdc as Row 2, until work measures approx. 20 in. (50 cm).
Fasten off yarn.

3 Sew the bag
With the right side facing you, fold the fabric in half widthways (so that the right sides are now together) and stitch the open side and bottom seams together. Turn the bag right side out.

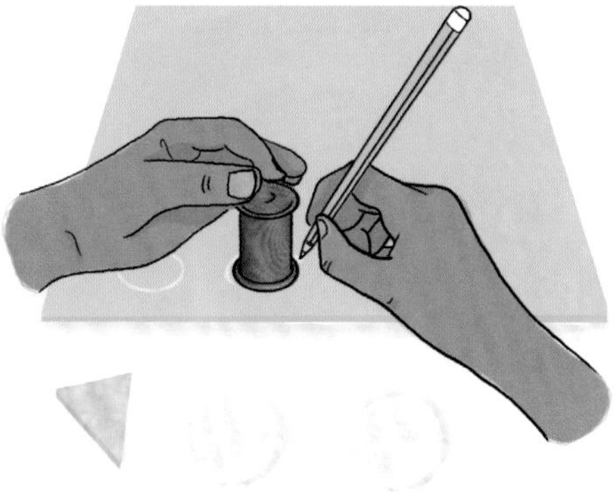

4 Make the eyes and beak

Cut out circles from the pieces of felt—you could draw around something to help you if you're not sure about cutting a circle freehand. Cut off the corner of a piece of felt to make a triangle for the beak.

Abbreviations (see page 19)

ch chain

hdc half double crochet

st(s) stitch(es)

Techniques (see pages 10–19)

Fastening off

Joining in a new color

Making fabric

Sewing on buttons

Sewing up

Turn

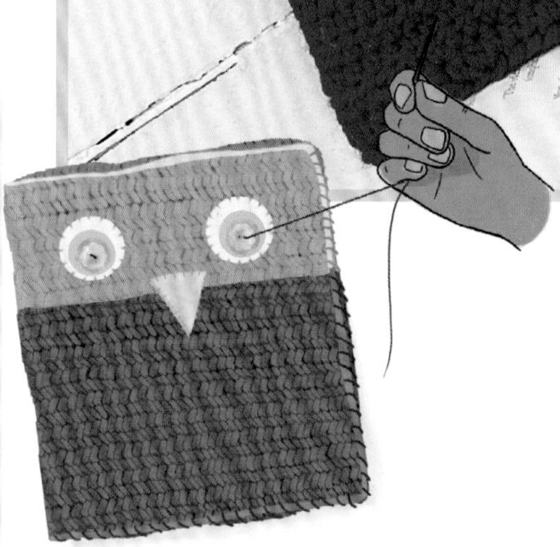

5 Add buttons

Sew the white felt circles for the eyes and the beak to the front of the bag using small overstitches and sewing thread. Attach the green circles to the eyes by sewing them in place with buttons.

6 Attach the straps

Using gray yarn and a darning needle, sew a strap to the top inner edge of each side of the bag, attaching it each end 2½ in. (6 cm) in from the sides. Make sure that the strap isn't twisted before you sew it in place.

Hat with earflaps

Keep warm and cozy in this snuggly hat. The earflaps are decorated with pompoms on strings, but you could leave them plain if you prefer.

You will need

1 x 1¾ oz (50 g) ball (81 yd/75 m) Sirdar Click Chunky with wool (70% acrylic, 30% wool), in each of:

Yarn A: shade 165, blue

Yarn B: shade 142, lamb

H/8 (5 mm) crochet hook

Darning needle

Cardboard

A round object with a diameter of 4 in. (10 cm) or a pompom maker

Measurements

Finished hat approx. 22½ in. (57 cm) unstretched

Gauge

Approx. 12 sts and 9 rows to 4 in. (10 cm) over hdc using H/8 (5 mm) hook, or size required to obtain correct gauge.

1 **Crochet the hat**
Using H/8 (5 mm) hook and yarn A, ch2.
Rnd 1: 6hdc in first ch made, join into a ring with a sl st.
Rnd 2: Ch2, 2hdc in each st around, join with a sl st into top of 2-ch. (12 hdc)
Rnd 3: Ch2, 2hdc in each st around, join with a sl st into top of 2-ch. (24 hdc)
Rnd 4: Ch2, [2hdc in next st, 1hdc] around, join with a sl st into top of 2-ch. (36 hdc)
Rnd 5: Ch2, [2hdc in next st, 2hdc] around, join with a sl st into top of 2-ch. (48 hdc)
Change to yarn B and work 1 rnd even in sc.
Change back to yarn A.
Rnd 7: Ch2, [2hdc in next st, 6hdc] around, join with a sl st into top of 2-ch. (54 hdc)
Change to yarn B and work 1 rnd even in sc.
Change back to yarn A.
Work 2 rnds even in hdc.
Change to yarn B.
Work 4 rnds even in hdc.
Change to yarn A and work 3 rows even in hdc.

2 **Crochet the earflap**
Work even for earflap as follows:
Row 1: 12hdc, turn, leaving rem sts unworked.
Row 2: Hdc2tog, hdc to last 2 sts, hdc2tog, turn. (10 hdc)
Rep last row until 4 sts rem.
Fasten off yarn.
Rejoin yarn A to 17th st along from last earflap and work as for first earflap.

Abbreviations (see page 19)

ch chain

hdc half double crochet

hdc2tog half double crochet 2 together

rep repeat

rem remain

rnd round

sc single crochet

sl st slip stitch

Techniques (see pages 10–19)

Fastening off

Making fabric

Turn

Working in the round

NOTE Hat is worked in complete rounds, do not turn throughout.

Earflaps are worked in rows, turn at the end of each row.

Yarn is not fastened off after each color change, and you do not need to join yarn to each new row once it has been joined in. Simply carry the yarn at the back of the work, and pick up and work the new yarn in the next stitch when instructed.

Have fun making pompoms

3 Crochet the border

Join yarn B to any point around edge of hat and work a row of sc evenly around entire edge, including earflaps. Do not turn. Work one further row in sc. Fasten off yarn.

4 Finishing

Use the darning needle to weave in the ends. Ask an adult to help you to lightly press the hat with an iron, placing a dish towel on top to protect the yarn if necessary.

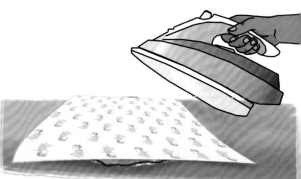

5 Make the pompoms

Make two multi-colored pompoms approx. 4 in. (10 cm) diameter, using strands of yarns A and B held together. You can either use a pompom maker or make your own. Draw around something with a diameter of about 4 in. (10 cm) onto two pieces of stiff cardstock or cardboard (a cereal carton works well). Draw a smaller circle inside (draw around a large button or a cotton reel). Cut out the larger circle then cut out the inner circle.

Keep the 2 circles held together and wrap the yarn through the ring, wrapping it closely together. Don't wrap it too tightly or it will be difficult to cut. When it is closely packed with yarn all the way around, carefully cut through the wraps of yarn around the edge of the rings. Slide a length of yarn between the rings and tie it tightly with a knot to hold all the strands together.

Remove the rings of the pompom maker and fluff up the pompom. You can trim any straggly ends with scissors to make a neat ball.

Make the ties

6 Crochet two chains for the ties, approx. 20 in. (50 cm) long and attach one to the bottom of each earflap. Sew the pompoms to the ties to finish.

Bootie slippers

Simple slippers—which are easily adaptable for your size of foot—are brilliant for keeping your toes cozy while you watch tv, chat online, or do your homework.

You will need

1 x 1¾ oz (50 g) ball (109 yd/100 m) Rico Essentials Soft Merino Aran (100% merino wool), in each of:

Yarn A: shade 020, light gray

Yarn B: shade 041, eucalyptus

Yarn C: shade 036, royal blue

Yarn D: shade 050, pistachio

Yarn E: shade 037, navy

Paper and pencil

H/8 (5 mm) and B/1 (2.5 mm) crochet hooks

Thick wool felt

Darning needle

Measurements

Adjustable to fit your own foot size.

Gauge

17sc and 16 rows to 4 in. (10 cm) over sc using H/8 (5 mm) hook, or size required to obtain correct gauge.

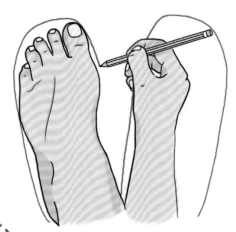

1 Make the slipper sole

Draw around your foot onto a piece of paper to get the basic shape and size of the sole—if one foot is larger than the other, draw around the larger one. Round off the shape so that it flows smoothly, and make it symmetrical so that either slipper fits either foot.

2 Cut out the felt

Pin your foot template to the felt and cut out two shapes. Punch holes all round the edge of the felt using a sharp needle or the end of your small crochet hook. Space the holes ¼ in. (5 mm) apart and ¼ in. (5 mm) in from the outside edge.

Abbreviations (see page 19)

ch chain

rep repeat

rnd round

sc single crochet

sc2tog single crochet 2 together

sl st slip stitch

Techniques (see pages 10–19)

Decreasing

Fastening off

Joining in a new color

Making fabric

Sewing up

Starting to work in the round

3 Crochet the slipper

Using the B/1 (2.5 mm) hook and yarn A, make a slip knot. Starting at the hole nearest the center of the heel, work 1sc in each of the holes around the edge of the felt sole. Join rnd with a sl st to first sc.

Change to H/8 (5 mm) hook.

Rnd 2: Ch1, 1sc in each st around, join with sl st to first sc.

Rep Rnd 2 four more times.

Rnd 7: Work in sc, decreasing 5 sts evenly over toe sts.

Change to yarn B and work one row even in sc without decreasing.

Change to yarn C.

Rnd 9: Work in sc, decreasing 5 sts evenly over toe sts.

Change to yarn D and work one row even in sc without decreasing.

Change to yarn E.

Rnd 11: Work in sc, decreasing 5 sts evenly over toe sts.

Fasten off yarn.

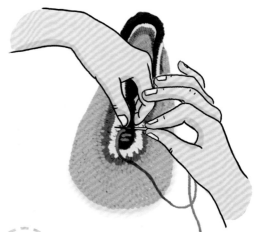

4 Finishing

Thread the darning needle with a length of yarn E and sew up the seam from the toe for 2 in. (5 cm) to join the top of the slipper.

No more boring slippers!

Rose book bag

This project uses single crochet throughout and is perfect as a book bag. You can make the flowers included in the pattern, or use any of the other flowers in the book to decorate your bag—try those from the Floral Purse on page 30, too.

You will need

Debbie Bliss Como (90% wool, 10% cashmere):

6 x 1¾ oz (50 g) balls (276 yd/252 m) in Yarn A: shade 24, silver

1 x 1¾ oz (50 g) ball (46 yd/42 m) in Yarn B: shade 18, lime

1 x 1¾ oz (50 g) ball (131 yd/120 m) Rowan Belle Organic DK (50% organic wool, 50% cotton) in Yarn C: shade 004, persimmon

1 x 1¾ oz (50 g) ball (103 yd/94 m) Rooster Almerino Aran (50% baby alpaca, 50% merino) in Yarn D: shade 306, gooseberry

M/13 (9 mm), K/11 (7 mm), and US 7 (4.5 mm) crochet hooks

Darning needle

Sewing needle and thread

Measurements

Bag approx. 13½ x 11½ in. (34 x 29 cm), handles 25 in. (64 cm)

Gauge

Exact gauge isn't important on this project.

1 Crochet the bag (make 2 pieces)
Using M/13 (9 mm) hook and yarn A, ch25.
Next row: Ch1, 1sc to end, turn.
Rep this row until bag measures 12½ in. (32 cm).
Fasten off yarn.

2 Crochet the edging
Work around top edge of bag. With the right side facing and using M/13 (9 mm) hook and yarn B, join yarn in a corner st, *ch3, sl st in 3rd ch from hook, skip 1 st, 1sc in next st; rep from * to end. Sl st into joining st.
Fasten off yarn.

3 Crochet the handles (make two)
Using K/11 (7 mm) hook and yarn A, ch5, turn, 1sc in second ch from hook, 1sc to end. (4 sts)
Next row: Ch1, 1sc in each st to end, turn. (4 sts)
Rep this row until handle measures approx. 26in. (66 cm).
Fasten off yarn.

Shopping with style!

Abbreviations (see page 19)

ch chain

ch sp chain space

cont continue

dc double crochet

rep repeat

rnd round

sc single crochet

st(s) stitch(es)

sl st slip stitch

Techniques (see pages 10–19)

Fastening off

Joining in a new color

Making fabric

Sewing up

Starting to work in the round

Turn

4 Crochet the flowers (make 4)

Using US 7 (4.5 mm) hook and yarn C, ch4, sl st into first ch to make a ring.

Rnd 1: *1sc, 1dc, 1sc into ring; rep from * 3 more times. (4 petals)

Rnd 2: *Ch2, from wrong side sl st into base of second sc of next petal (pick up 2 loops); rep from * 3 more times. Slip last st into first sl st. (4 loops)

Rnd 3: *4dc in next 2-ch sp, sl st in same ch sp; rep from * 3 more times.
Fasten off yarn.

Rnd 4: Continue in yarn C. Work into back of petals and picking up two loops, join yarn at base of highest point of previous round, *ch3, sl st into middle of base of next petal; rep from * 3 more times, slip last st into joining st.

Rnd 5: *8dc in next 3-ch sp, sl st in next 3-ch sp; rep from * 3 more times, slip last st into joining st.
Fasten off yarn.
Change to yarn D.

Rnd 6: Working into back of petals and picking up two loops, join yarn into middle of base of petal (next 8 dc) of previous round, *ch3, sl st into middle of base of next petal; rep from * 3 more times, slip last st into joining st.

Rnd 7: *10dc in 3-ch sp, sl st in same 3-ch sp; rep from * 3 more times.
Fasten off yarn.

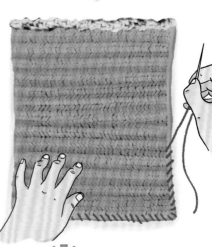

5 Sew the bag

With wrong sides facing, use a darning needle and matching yarn to sew the front and back together with whip stitch, sewing up the side and bottom seams, and leaving the top open.

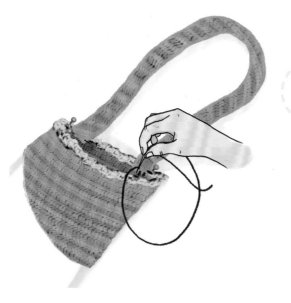

6 Attach the handles

Place a pin 1 in. (2.5 cm) from each outside seam on the top of the bag as a marker. Position the ends of the handles approx. 2 in. (5 cm) down into the bag, aligning the outside edge of the handle with the pin. Stitch the handle in place and repeat on the same side with the other end of the handle (make sure the handle isn't twisted). Repeat for the second handle on the other side of the bag.

 **Attach the flowers**
Sew each flower to the front of
the bag, just below the handles,
keeping your stitches hidden at the back
of the flower.

CHAPTER 2

Jewelry

Chain necklace

You only need to know how to make a chain to make this fun and colorful necklace. The necklace can be made in any length—you could make shorter ones as bracelets or anklets, or make it longer to wear as a decorative belt. Remember to string all your beads onto the yarn before you start!

You will need

1 x 1¾ oz (50 g) ball (142 yd/130 m) Rico Essentials Cotton DK (100% mercerized cotton) in shade 01, rose

US 6 (4 mm) crochet hook

12 wooden or plastic shaped beads, approx. ½–¾ in. (1–1.5 cm) diameter

Measurements

Approx. 55 in. (140 cm), but you can make yours to any length

Gauge

Exact gauge isn't important for this project.

Abbreviations (see page 19)

ch chain

rep repeat

sl st slip stitch

Techniques (see pages 10–19)

Fastening off

1 **Thread the beads**
Attach the darning needle to the end of the yarn and thread it through 12 beads. Make a slip knot in the yarn end before the beads and place it on the hook.

Beads galore!

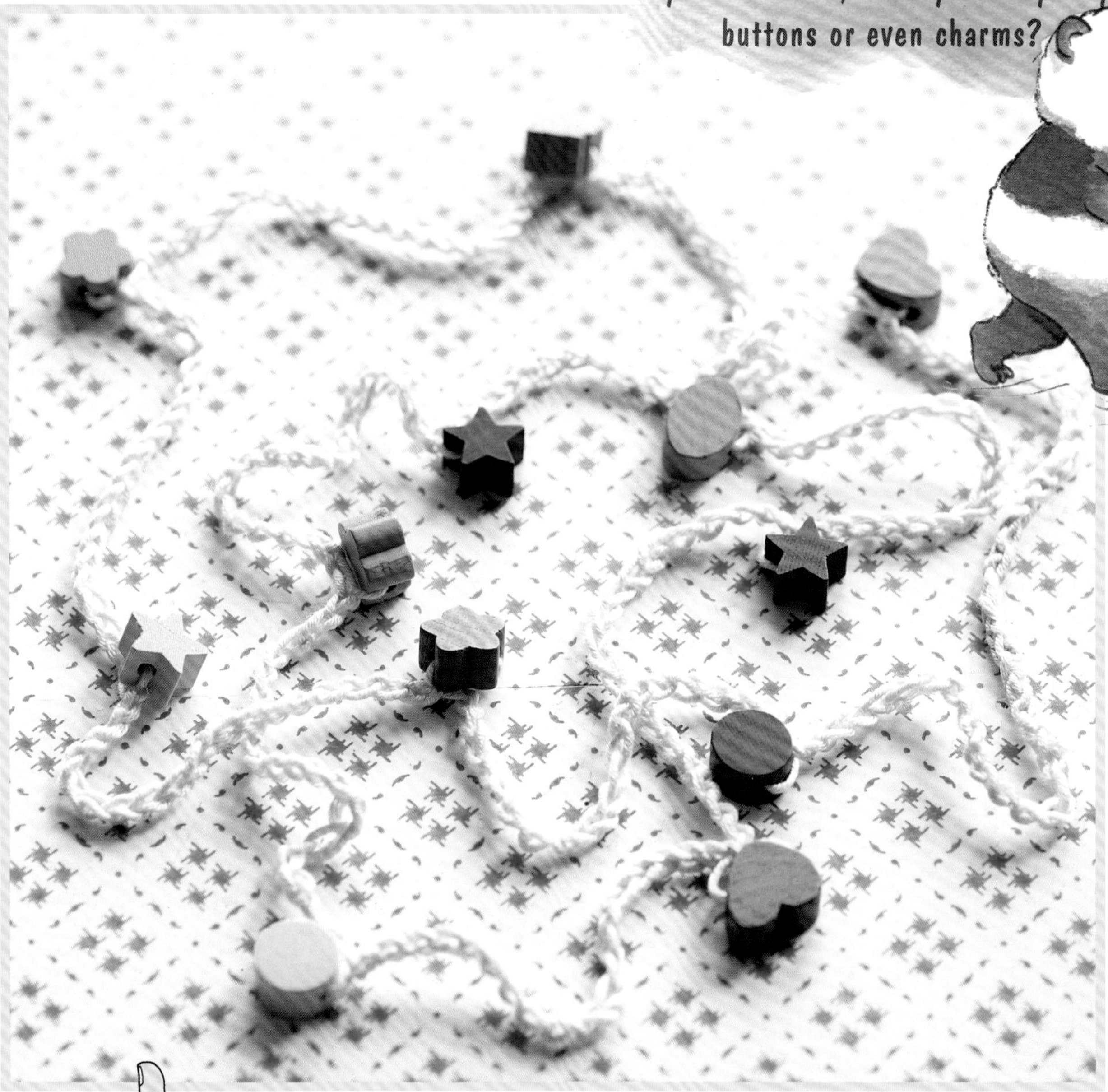

You can use any type of bead for your necklace, or why not try tiny buttons or even charms?

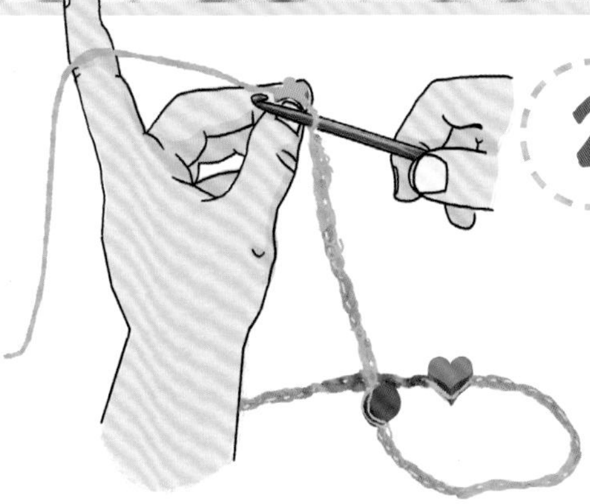

2 **Crochet the chain**

Using US 6 (4 mm) hook, *ch20, bring bead up to hook, ch around bead; rep from * until all beads are used, ch20, sl st in first ch made.

Fasten off the yarn and weave in the ends.

Headband

A basic strip of crochet can be easily turned into a headband, with a cute bow to hide the seam and add extra prettiness.

○ ○ ☺

You will need

1 x 1¾ oz (50 g) ball (191 yd/175 m) Sirdar Snuggly Kisses DK (55% nylon, 45% acrylic), in shade 0754, pink

D/3 (3.25 mm) crochet hook

Darning needle

Measurements

Headband is approx. 2¼ in. (5.5 cm) wide and to fit head approx. 17¼(19:20½) in. [44(48:52) cm] around, although it is easy to adapt to fit your own head

Gauge

Approx. 21 sts and 14 rows to 4 in. (10 cm) over hdc using D/3 (3.25 mm) hook, or size required to obtain correct gauge.

1 ### Crochet the headband

Using D/3 (3.25 mm) hook, ch14.

Row 1: 1hdc in 2nd ch from hook, then 1hdc in each ch to end of row, turn. (12 hdc)

Row 2: Ch2, 1hdc in each st to end of row, turn.

Rep last row until headband is approx. 17¼(19:20½) in. [44(48:52) cm] long, or desired head circumference, allowing for stretch.

Fasten off yarn.

2 ### Crochet the bow

Using D/3 (3.25 mm) hook, ch16.

Row 1: 1hdc in 2nd ch from hook, then 1hdc in each ch to end of row, turn. (14 hdc)

Row 2: Ch2, 1hdc in each st to end of row, turn.

Rep last row until strip is approx. 4 in. (10 cm) long.

Fasten off yarn.

Using D/3 (3.25 mm) hook, ch8.

Row 1: 1hdc in 2nd ch from hook, then 1hdc in each ch to end of row, turn. (6 hdc)

Row 2: Ch2, 1hdc in each st to end of row, turn.

Rep last row until strip is approx. 4½ in. (11 cm) long.

Fasten off yarn.

Perfect for dance class

3 Sew together

Sew the ends of the headband together to make a circle, using a darning needle and whip stitch.

Abbreviations (see page 19)

ch chain

hdc half double crochet

rep repeat

sl st slip stitch

Techniques (see pages 10–19)

Fastening off

Making fabric

Sewing up

Turn

4 Attach the bow

Position the larger bow strip centered over the seam on the headband and sew it in place in the middle along the edge for about 1 in. (2.5 cm) on each side. Wrap the small bow strip around the center of the larger bow strip and headband, sewing the ends together at back of the headband to create a gathered bow.

Flowers

It's so easy to work in the round and create fast and simply stunning pins or hairclips with these pretty flowers. Adorn these little lovelies with buttons or beads for added sparkle.

Crochet the large daisy

Using E/4 (3.5 mm) hook and yarn A, ch6 and join into a ring with a sl st.

Rnd 1: 20sc into ring, join rnd with a sl st.
Fasten off yarn A.
Join yarn B to any sc with a sl st.
Rnd 2: Ch20, [sl st in next sc, ch20] around, join last petal to bottom of first ch with a sl st.
Fasten off yarn and weave in ends.
Attach a pin back, safety pin or hairclip to the back of the flower with a few stitches over and over the fastening, using a sewing needle and thread. You could add buttons or beads to the front, too.

The flowers use very small amounts of yarn, so they're perfect for using up left-overs.

Abbreviations (see page 19)

ch chain

dc double crochet

rep repeat

sc single crochet

sl st slip stitch

sp space

Techniques (see pages 10–19)

Fastening off

Joining in a new color

Turn

Sewing on buttons

Starting to work in the round

NOTE Daisies and small flowers are worked in complete rounds, do not turn throughout.

Loopy flower is worked in rows.

(2) Crochet the small daisy

Using E/4 (3.5 mm) hook and yarn A, ch6 and join into a ring with a sl st.

Rnd 1: 20sc into ring, join into top of first sc with a sl st. Fasten off yarn A.

Join yarn B to any sc with a sl st.

Rnd 2: Ch10, [skip 1 sc, sl st in next sc, ch10] around, join last petal to bottom of first ch with a sl st.

Fasten off yarn and weave in ends.

Attach a pin back, safety pin, or hairclip to the back of the flower with a few stitches over and over the fastening, using a sewing needle and thread. You could add buttons or beads to the front, too.

3 Crochet the loopy flower

Using E/4 (3.5 mm) hook and yarn C, ch5.

Row 1: 1sc in 2nd ch from hook, 1sc in each ch to end of row, turn. (4 sc)

Row 2: Ch30, 1sc in sc at base of ch, sc to end of row, turn.

Row 3: Ch1, sc to end of row, turn.

Row 4: Ch30, 1sc in sc at base of ch, sc to end of row, turn.

Rep Rows 3–4 eight times more.
Change to yarn D.

Next row: Ch1, sc to end of row, turn.

Next row: Ch25, 1sc in sc at base of ch, sc to end of row, turn.

Next row: Ch1, sc to end of row, turn.

Rep last two rows 9 times more.

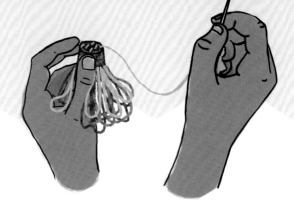

Change to yarn E.

Next row: Ch1, sc to end of row, turn.

Next row: Ch20, 1sc in sc at base of ch, sc to end of row, turn.

Next row: Ch1, sc to end of row, turn.

Rep last two rows 9 times more.
Fasten off yarn.

Roll up strip with smaller loops in the middle and secure in place by sewing together through the sc section at the back.

Attach a pin back, safety pin, or hairclip to the back of the flower with a few stitches over and over the fastening, using a sewing needle and thread.

4 Crochet the small flower

Using E/4 (3.5 mm) hook and yarn F, ch3.

Rnd 1: 5sc in first ch, join with a sl st into top of first st.

Rnd 2: 2sc in each st around, join with a sl st into top of first st. (10 sc)

Rnd 3: [1sc, 2sc in next st] around, join with a sl st into top of first st. (15 sc)
Fasten off yarn F.

Join yarn G to any sc with a sl st.

Rnd 4: Ch1, 2dc in each of next 2 sts, [1sc, 2dc in each of next 2 sts] to end of rnd, join with a sl st in top of 1-ch. (5 petals made)

Fasten off yarn and weave in ends.

Attach a pin back, safety pin, or hairclip to the back of the flower with a few stitches over and over the fastening, using a sewing needle and thread. You could also add buttons or beads to the front, too.

Heart and star hairclips

Crochet is the perfect way to cover boring hairclips and barettes in a favorite color. Add a cute heart or star to really make them shine.

You will need

1 x 3½ oz (100 g) ball (306 yd/280 m) DMC Petra no 3 (100% long staple cotton), in each of:

Yarn A: shade 5321, red

Yarn B: shade 53904, ice blue

Yarn C: shade 53900, green

D/3 (3.25 mm) crochet hook

Hairclips or plain barettes

Sewing needle and matching thread

Measurements

One size, hearts and stars approx. 1 in. (2.5 cm) wide

Gauge

Exact gauge isn't important for this project.

1 Crochet the hairclip

Using D/3 (3.25 mm) hook and any color, join yarn to the point of the hairclip with a sl st. Work sc round the clip, through the center hole, to cover it, leaving the broad end unworked. Fasten off yarn.

2 Crochet the heart

Rnd 1: Ch2, 9sc in 2nd ch from hook, join into a ring with a sl st.

Rnd 2: Ch1, 1sc in next st, [1hdc, 5dc, 1hdc] all into next st, sl st in next st, [1hdc, 5dc, 1hdc] all into next st, sc to end of rnd, join with a sl st into first ch. Fasten off yarn.

3 Crochet the star

Rnd 1: Ch2, 10sc in 2nd ch from hook, join with a sl st into top of 2-ch.

Rnd 2: [Ch2, 1dc in next st, ch2, sl st in next st] 5 times. Fasten off yarn.

Accessorize with cute clips

ch chain

dc double crochet

hdc half double crochet

sc single crochet

sl st slip stitch

st stitch

Techniques (see pages 10–19)

Fastening off

(4) **Finish the hairclip**
Sew the heart or star to the wide end of the clip to hide the uncovered part, using a sewing needle and matching sewing thread.

Bracelets

These simple bracelet tubes can be adapted to fit you perfectly. Make lots of them in different colors to go with all your favorite clothes.

You will need

1 x 1¾ oz (50 g) ball (104 yd/95 m) Sirdar Snuggly Baby Bamboo (80% bamboo, 20% wool), in each of:

Yarn A: shade 162, toy box red

Yarn B: shade 160, paint box pink

Yarn C: shade 161, baby berries purple

Yarn D: shade 159, jack-in-the-box turquoise

E/4 (3.5 mm) crochet hook

Stitch marker

Darning needle

Measurements

To fit you!

Gauge

Exact gauge isn't important for this project.

1 Crochet the bracelet

Using E/4 (3.5 mm) hook and any yarn, ch8, join into a ring with a sl st into top of first ch.

Rnd 1: Ch1, 1sc (blo) in each ch around, do not join rnd.

Rnd 2: 1sc (blo) in each ch around, do not join rnd.

Rep last rnd until bracelet measures approx. 7 in. (18 cm), or length to fit your wrist allowing for stretch over hand. Fasten off yarn.

2 Finishing the bracelet

Thread the tail end of the yarn onto a darning needle and sew the two open ends together neatly to form a circle.

Groovy bracelets for every day!

Abbreviations (see page 19)

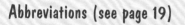

blo back loop only

ch chain

rep repeat

sc single crochet

sl st slip stitch

Techniques (see pages 10–19)

Fastening off

Marking rounds with a stitch marker

Starting to work in the round

NOTE Bracelets are worked in continuous spiral rounds, do not turn throughout and do not join rounds.

Felted cherry pin

These cherries are very quick and really cute. They are small and a little bit fiddly, but the stitch is very simple—so once you've mastered crocheting in the round, give them a go.

You will need

1 x 3½ oz (100 g) hank (220 yd/ 200 m) Cascade 220 DK (100% Peruvian wool) in each of:

Yarn A: shade 8414, bright red

Yarn B: shade 0980, pesto

E/4 (3.5 mm) crochet hook

Darning needle

Sewing needle and thread

Small pin back

Measurements

Approx. 2¾ in. (7 cm) wide x 3 in. (7.5 cm) long

Gauge

Exact gauge isn't important on this project.

1 **Crochet the cherries (make two)**
Using E/4 (3.5 mm) hook and yarn A, ch2.
Rnd 1: 6sc in second ch from hook.
Rnd 2: 2sc in each st. (12 sc)
Rnd 3: 1sc in each st. (12 sc)
Stuff cherry with scraps of red yarn.
Rnd 4: Sc2tog around. (6 sc)
Continue to sc2tog until hole closes.
Fasten off yarn and weave in ends.

2 **Crochet the stalk (make one)**
Using E/4 (3.5 mm) hook and yarn B, ch20.
Fasten off yarn.

3 **Crochet the leaves (make two)**
Using E/4 (3.5 mm) hook and yarn B, ch8, sl st in second ch from hook, 1sc, 1hdc, 1dc, 1hdc, 1sc, sl st in last ch.
Working on other side of ch, sl st in second ch from hook, 1sc in next st, 1hdc, 1dc, 1hdc, 1sc, sl st.
Fasten off yarn.

Abbreviations (see page 19)

ch chain

hdc half double crochet

rnd round

sc single crochet

sc2tog single crochet 2 together

sl st slip stitch

Techniques (see pages 10–19)

Fastening off

Starting to work in the round

So sweet and easy!

4 Sew the cherry

Using a darning needle and matching yarn, sew one end of the stalk to each cherry. Find the center of the stalk and sew the leaves to the top.

To felt well, the cherries must be made in 100% wool.

5 Felting

Ask an adult to help you use the washing machine. Put the cherries in a pillowcase or laundry bag and wash in the washing machine on a hot wash, twice (include a large towel or two to help). When felted, the wool will be thicker and the crochet will have shrunk a little. Let the pin dry.

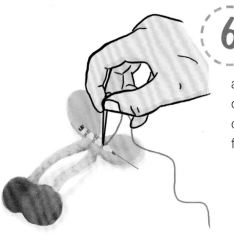

6 Finish the pin

Attach a pin back to the reverse of the leaves using a sewing needle and thread. Take a few stitches over and over the fastening, making sure that you can't see the stitches or the pin back from the front.

Princess tiara

A simple-to-make tiara fit for any little princess. We've sewn on pearls, but you can use beads or sew-on jewels if you prefer.

○ ○ ☺

You will need

1 x ¾ oz (20 g) ball (164 yd/150 m) DMC Metallic Crochet Thread (60% viscose, 40% metalized polyester), in shade L168, silver

C/2 (2.75 mm) crochet hook

Darning needle

Headband

Beads for embellishment

Beading or thin sewing needle and thread

Measurements

Headband to fit wearer's head; crocheted section is approx. ¾ in. (2 cm) high

Gauge

Exact gauge isn't important for this project.

1 Crochet the tiara

Using C/2 (2.75 mm) hook, attach yarn to headband and work 42sc around the center section of the headband, turn.
Next row: 1sc, [ch5, skip 3 sts, 1sc in next st] 5 times, ch6, skip 4 sts, 1sc in next st, ch7, skip 5 sts, 1sc in next st, ch6, skip 4 sts, 1sc in next st, [ch5, skip 3 sts, 1sc in next st] 5 times, turn.

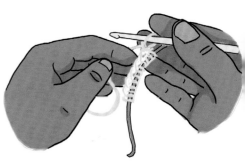

Next row: [7sc in next 5-ch sp, sl st in sc] 5 times, 9sc in next ch sp, sl st in sc, 11sc in next ch sp, sl st in sc, 9sc in next ch sp, sl st in sc [7sc in next 5-ch sp, sl st in sc] 5 times.
Fasten off yarn.

2 Adding beads

If you'd like to add some extra jewels to your tiara you can attach beads to the crochet. Thread a beading or sewing needle with thread and knot the end. Bring the needle out in the position where you would like your bead. Thread a bead onto the needle and down the thread. Take the needle back in close to where it emerged, so that the bead sits on the headband. Take a few more stitches through the bead to secure it.

Abbreviations (see page 19)

ch chain

ch sp chain space

rep repeat

sc single crochet

sl st slip stitch

sp space

Techniques (see pages 10–19)

Fastening off

Turn

For a simple version, simply work a row of single crochet then finish off.

CHAPTER 3
....

Bedroom Essentials

Floral curtain tie-backs

These curtain ties use very little yarn, so you can use up scraps of any type left over from another project. Simply fasten them over a hook behind the curtains to add some pretty styling to your bedroom.

You will need

1 x 1¾ oz (50 g) ball (120 yd/110 m) Debbie Bliss Cashmerino DK (55% merino wool, 33% microfiber, 12% cashmere) in Yarn A: shade 011, green

1 x 1¾ oz (50 g) ball (124 yd/112.5 m) Rooster Almerino DK (50% baby alpaca, 50% merino wool) in Yarn B: shade 211, Brighton Rock

US 6 (4 mm) crochet hook

Darning needle

Measurements

Makes two tie-backs each approx. 43 in. (110 cm) long

Gauge

Exact gauge isn't important for this project.

1 Crochet the petal flowers (make 10)

Using US 6 (4 mm) hook and yarn A, ch6, join with sl st into first ch. Make 16sc into ring, joining tail into each sc around ring, join with a sl st into top of first st.
Change to yarn B.
*Ch3, 1dc in each of next 2 sts, ch3, sl st in next st; rep from * 4 more times. (5 petals)
Fasten off yarn.
Pull tail to close up center hole and sew in ends.

2 Crochet the small roses (make 4)

Using US 6 (4 mm) hook and yarn B, ch48.
Petals 1–3: Skip 3 ch, 1dc in each of next 2 ch, ch2, sl st in next ch, *ch3, 1dc in each of next 2 ch, ch2, sl st in next ch; rep from * to end once more. (3 petals)
Petals 4–6: *Ch4, 1tr in each of next 4 ch, ch3, sl st in next ch; rep from * twice more.
Petals 7–9: *Ch4, 1tr in each of next 6 ch, ch3, sl st in next ch; rep from * twice more.
Fasten off yarn.

Abbreviations (see page 19)

ch chain

dc double crochet

dtr double treble

rep repeat

sc single crochet

st(s) stitch(es)

sl st slip stitch

tr treble

Techniques (see pages 10–19)

Fastening off

Turn

NOTE Each tie-back has two small roses, one large rose and five petal flowers.

 Crochet the large roses (make 2)

Using US 6 (4 mm) hook and yarn B, ch99.

Petals 1–4: Skip 3 ch, 1dc in each of next 2 ch, ch2, sl st in next ch, [ch3, 1dc in each of next 2 ch, ch2, sl st in next ch] 3 times.

Petals 5–8: [Ch4, 1tr in each of next 4 ch, ch3, sl st in next ch] 4 times.

Petals 9–12: [Ch4, 1tr in each of next 6 ch, ch3, sl st in next ch] 4 times.

Petals 13–16: [Ch5, 1dtr in each of next 8 ch, ch4, sl st in next ch] 4 times.

Fasten off yarn.

4 Make up the roses

To make roses, ask an adult to help you press the petals flat with an iron. Starting with smaller petals, coil the petals round, keeping the base flat at the chain edge, and stitch in place as you go.

5 Make the tie-back chain

Using yarn A, make two lengths of chain for each tie-back, each 21 in. (54 cm) long.
Fasten off yarn.

6 Attach the flowers

Attach one end of one chain to the back of one small rose, leave a 4 in. (10 cm) gap then attach the chain to the back of a large rose. Make a 1 in. (2.5 cm) loop at other end of chain and stitch it in place.

7 Join the tie-back chains

Attach one end of the second chain to the back of the other small rose. Leave a 3 in. (7.5 cm) gap and cross the second chain over the first chain on the back of the large rose. Attach in place, so the chains are secured and crossed at the back. Make a 1 in. (2.5 cm) loop at the other end of the second chain and stitch it in place.

8 Attach the petal flowers

Place five petal flowers along the chains where they will be visible, leaving a 1 in. (2.5 cm) gap between each. Sew the petal flowers to the chain. Use the loops to attach the tie-back to a hook. Repeat steps 5 to 8 to make the second tie-back.

Storage jars

Make these covers for jars, vases, and cans to store pens, pencils, crochet hooks—or fill them with water to display flowers with colorful style.

You will need

1 x 1¾ oz (50 g) ball (120 yd/112 m) Artesano Soft Merino Superwash DK (100% merino superwash), in each of:

Yarn A: shade 1291, sea blue

Yarn B: shade 5167, teal

Yarn C: shade 2083, fuchsia

Yarn D: shade 6315, lime green

Yarn E: shade SFN10, cream

Yarn F: shade 7254, sand yellow

E/4 (3.5 mm) crochet hook

Darning needle

Assorted jars and containers

Measurements

To fit tubular storage containers of approx. 2 in., 2¾ in., and 3½ in. (5 cm, 7 cm, and 9 cm) in diameter, and of any height

Gauge

Approx. 18 sts and 26 rows to 4 in. (10 cm) in sc using E/4 (3.5 mm) hook, or size required to obtain correct gauge.

1 Crochet the cover

Begin all covers from Rnd 1. For 2 in. (5 cm) size, work to Rnd 5 and then work from the all sizes instruction; for 2¾ in. (7 cm) size, work to Rnd 7 and then work from all sizes instruction; and for 3½ in. (9 cm) size, work all rows before completing from "all sizes" instruction.

Begin with yarn A and then work 1 or 2 row stripes alternately of all colors.

Using E/4 (3.5 mm) hook and yarn A, ch2.

Rnd 1: 6sc in first ch, join into a ring with a sl st.

Rnd 2: 2sc in each st around, join with a sl st into top of first st. (12 sc)

Rnd 3: [1sc, 2sc in next st] around. (18 sc)

Rnd 4: [2sc, 2sc in next st] around. (24 sc)

Rnd 5: [3sc, 2sc in next st] around. (30 sc)

Rnd 6: [4sc, 2sc in next st] around. (36 sc)

Rnd 7: [5sc, 2sc in next st] around. (42 sc)

Rnd 8: [6sc, 2sc in next st] around, join with a sl st into top of first st. (48 sc)

Rnd 9: [7sc, 2sc in next st] around, join rnd with a sl st. (54 sc)

Rnd 10: [8sc, 2sc in next st] around, join rnd with a sl st. (60 sc)

All sizes

Next rnd: Ch1, 1sc in each st around, join rnd with a sl st. Continue even in sc on these sts until desired height of jar is reached, striping as you wish.

Fasten off yarn.

Keep your pencils tidy!

Abbreviations (see page 19)

blo back loop only

ch chain

sc single crochet

rnd round

sl st slip stitch

Techniques (see pages 10–19)

Fastening off

Joining in a new color

Starting to work in the round

NOTE Pieces are worked in the round, do not turn throughout.

2 **Finishing the cover**
Use the darning needle to weave in the loose ends on the wrong side, then turn the cover right side out.

3 **Cover your jar**
Slip the crocheted "cozy" over a jar or vase and fill with pens and pencils or a pretty bunch of flowers.

Zigzag bolster

A crazily striped bolster for your bed. Have fun mixing and matching all your favorite colors.

1 Crochet the bolster

Using US 6 (4 mm) hook and yarn A, ch98.

Row 1: 2sc in 2nd ch from hook, *1sc in each of next 7 ch, skip 1 ch, 1sc in each of next 7 ch, 3sc in next ch; rep from * to end, but work 2sc in last ch instead of 3sc, turn.

Row 2: Ch1, 2sc in first st, *7sc, skip next 2 sc, 7sc, 3sc in next stitch; rep from * to end, but work 2sc in last st instead of 3sc, turn.

Rep Row 2 for pattern, changing color after every four rows, until work measures approx. 19 in. (48 cm) long.

Fasten off yarn.

2 Sew together

Weave in the ends. Sew the piece together along the two long edges, fitting the peaks and troughs of the zigzag into each other, using a darning needle and whip stitch and a matching yarn.

Soft, cozy and funky!

You will need

1 x 1¾ oz (50 g) ball (104 yd/95 m) Sirdar Snuggly Baby Bamboo (80% bamboo, 20% wool), in each of:

Yarn A: shade 144, tom thumb green

Yarn B: shade 157, yellow submarine

Yarn C: shade 149, scooter blue

Yarn D: shade 159, jack-in-the-box turquoise

Yarn E: shade 161, baby berries purple

Yarn F: shade 160, paint box pink

Yarn G: shade 162, toy box red

Yarn H: shade 126, rocking horse red

Yarn I: shade 134, babe pink

US 6 (4 mm) crochet hook

Darning needle

Fiberfill stuffing, or bolster pad measuring 15½ in. (39 cm) long and 19½ in. (49 cm) in circumference

½ yd (½ m) fabric

A round object to draw around, like a plate, about 6 in. (15 cm) in diameter

Fabric marker pen

Sewing needle and matching thread

Measurements

Approx. 14 in. (36 cm) wide

Gauge

15 sts and 15 rows to 4 in. (10 cm) in zigzag pattern using US 6 (4 mm) hook, or size required to obtain correct gauge.

Abbreviations (see page 19)

ch chain

rep repeat

rnd round

sc single crochet

sc2tog single crochet 2 together

sl st slip stitch

st(s) stitch(es)

Techniques (see pages 10–19)

Fastening off

Joining in a new color

Turn

Sewing up

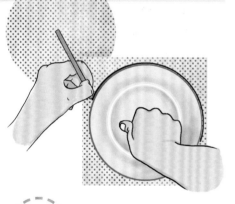

4 Sew the end

Fold the edge of the fabric circles over to the wrong side by about ½ in. (1 cm) and ask an adult to help you press them with an iron. Sew a circle of fabric to one end of the bolster using a sewing needle and thread and small overstitches.

3 Cut out the fabric

Put a plate or a round object of about 6 in. (15 cm) in diameter onto the wrong side of your fabric and draw round it to make two circles. Cut the circles out.

5 Finish the bolster

Either fill the bolster with fiberfill stuffing until it is firm or insert a bolster pad. Sew the remaining circle of fabric to the open end of the bolster as you did in step 4.

Colorful bowl

This small bowl can be used to hold items on your dresser or desk, like jewelry, paper clips, hairclips, or tiny toys. You could even make several bowls in different colors to liven up your room!

You will need

1 x 1¾ oz (50 g) ball (131 yd/120 m) Patons Diploma Gold DK (55% wool, 25% acrylic, 20% nylon) in Yarn A: shade 06125, apple green

Small amount of Stylecraft Special DK (100% acrylic) in Yarn B: shade 1068, turquoise

E/4 (3.5 mm) crochet hook

Stitch marker

Darning needle

Measurements

Our bowl measured about 4 in. (10 cm); however, the bowl can be made in any size

Gauge

Exact gauge isn't important for this project.

1 Crochet the bowl

Using E/4 (3.5 mm) hook and yarn A, ch2, 6sc in 2nd ch from hook.

Rnd 1: 2sc in each sc. (12 sts)

Rnd 2: *1sc in first sc, 2sc in next sc; rep from * to end. (18 sts)

Rnd 3: *1sc in each of next 2 sc, 2sc in next sc; rep from * to end. (24 sts)

Rnd 4: *1sc in each of next 3 sc, 2sc in next sc; rep from * to end. (30 sts)

Rnd 5: *1sc in each of next 4 sc, 2sc in next sc; rep from * to end. (36 sts)

Rnd 6: *1sc in each of next 5 sc, 2sc in next sc; rep from * to end. (42 sts)

Rnd 7: *1sc in each of next 6 sc, 2sc in next sc; rep from * to end. (48 sts)

Rnd 8: *1sc in each of next 7 sc, 2sc in next sc; rep from * to end. (54 sts)

Rnd 9: *1sc in each of next 8 sc, 2sc in next sc; rep from * to end. (60 sts)

Rnd 10: *1sc in each of next 9 sc, 2sc in next sc; rep from * to end. (66 sts)

Rnds 11–15: 1sc in each sc. (66 sts)

Change to yarn B.

Rnds 16–17: 1sc in each sc. (66 sts)

Fasten off yarn. Use the darning needle to weave in the tail ends.

Stylish storage for all your bits and bobs!

Abbreviations (see page 19)

....

ch chain

rep repeat

rnd round

sc single crochet

sl st slip stitch

st(s) stitch(es)

Techniques (see pages 10–19)

....

Fastening off

Marking rounds with a stitch marker

Starting to work in the round

This project is made in the round;
be sure to use a stitch marker to
mark the first stitch of
the round throughout.

Knickerbocker glory bunting

Bunting is a lovely, happy way to brighten up your bedroom or you could string it up in the garden or kitchen for a birthday celebration in style!

You will need

1 x 1¾ oz (50 g) ball (123 yd/112 m) King Cole Merino Blend DK (100% merino wool) in each of:

shade 5, sky

shade 55, gold

shade 94, dusky pink

shade 787, fuchsia

1 x 1¾ oz (50 g) ball (120 yd/110 m) Debbie Bliss Cashmerino DK (55% merino wool, 33% microfiber, 12% cashmere) in each of:

shade 017, lilac

shade 029, light green

1 x 1¾ oz (50 g) ball (131 yd/120 m) Rowan Belle Organic DK (50% organic wool, 50% cotton) in shade 004, persimmon

US 6 (4 mm) crochet hook

Darning needle

Measurements

Each flag approx. 7 in. (18 cm) across top edge

Gauge

Exact gauge isn't important for this project.

1 Crochet the flags

Make 6, or as many as required, in different colors with contrast edgings.
Using US 6 (4 mm) hook and flag main color, ch26.
Row 1: 1sc in 2nd ch from hook, 1sc in each ch to end, turn. (25 sts)
Row 2: Ch1, sc2tog, 1sc in each st to end, turn.
Rep row 2 until 2 sts remain, sc2tog.
Fasten off yarn.

2 Crochet the edging

With right sides facing, join in first contrast color into top right corner st, ch 3, make 24dc along top edge.
Fasten off yarn.
With right sides facing, join next contrast color in top left corner, ch1, work 26sc along first side, 3sc in corner st, 26sc along other side ending with a sl st into top of first st.
Fasten off yarn.

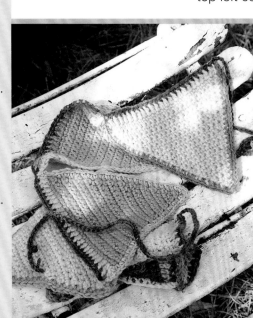

3 Join the flags

With a contrasting color, ch70. With right sides facing, join ch to first flag with sl st in right-hand corner, ch1, *1sc in between each dc across top of flag to end, join next flag with sl st into top right-hand corner; rep from * to end for each flag, sl st into last corner st of last flag. Ch70. Fasten off yarn.

Abbreviations (see page 19)

ch chain

dc double crochet

rep repeat

rnd round

sc single crochet

sc2tog single crochet 2 together

sl st slip stitch

st(s) stitch(es)

Techniques (see pages 10–19)

Fastening off

Joining in a new color

Turn

4 Sew in the ends

Using a darning needle at the back of the bunting, stitch to secure the joins in between each flag using the loose ends of yarn. Ask an adult to help you to press each flag gently with an iron.

Party time!

Sausage dog draft excluder

Keep your bedroom cozy on cold winter evenings by placing this dog by your door to stop drafts coming underneath, or fill the dog with PVC beanbag granules and use him as a doorstop.

You will need

1 x 1¾ oz (50 g) ball (81 yd/75 m) Sirdar Click Chunky with wool, (70% acrylic, 30% wool), in each of:

Yarn A: shade 148, bud

Yarn B: shade 163, really red

Yarn C: shade 171, blueberry

H/8 (5 mm) crochet hook

Fiberfill stuffing

Red felt for ears, legs, tail and nose

White felt for eyes

Buttons for eyes

Sewing needle and thread

Darning needle

Measurements

Approx. 27 in. (68.5 cm) long

Gauge

Exact gauge isn't important for this project but make sure that you crochet tightly so that the stuffing does not show.

① Crochet the dog

Using H/8 (5 mm) hook and yarn A, ch2.

Rnd 1: 6sc in first ch made, join with a sl st into top of first st.

Rnd 2: 2sc in each sc around, join with a sl st into top of first st. (12 sc)

Rnd 3: [2sc in next st, 1sc] around, join with a sl st into top of first st. (18 sc)

Rnd 4: [2sc in next st, 2sc] around, join with a sl st into top of first st. (24 sc)

Rnd 5: [2sc in next st, 3sc] around, join with a sl st into top of first st. (30 sc)

Rnd 6: [2sc in next st, 4sc] around, join with a sl st into top of first st. (36 sc)

Rnd 7: [2sc in next st, 5sc] around, join with a sl st into top of first st. (42 sc)

Rnd 8: [2sc in next st, 6sc] around, join with a sl st into top of first st. (48 sc)

Work 4 rows even in sc without increasing.

Change to yarn B and work 2 rows even.

Change to yarn C and work 2 rows even.

Change to yarn A and work 2 rows even.

Cont even on these 48 sts until dog is approx. 27 in. (68.5 cm) long, striping as established, then if necessary, change back to yarn A.

Stuff the body through the open end, with the hook still attached, and then begin to decrease as follows:

Rnd 1: [Sc2tog, 6sc] around, join with a sl st into first st. (42 sc)

Rnd 2: [Sc2tog, 5sc] around, join with a sl st into first st. (36 sc)

Rnd 3: [Sc2tog, 4sc] around, join with a sl st into first st. (30 sc)

Rnd 4: [Sc2tog, 3sc] around, join with a sl st into first st. (24 sc)

Rnd 5: [Sc2tog, 2sc] around, join with a sl st into first st. (18 sc)

Rnd 6: [Sc2tog, 1sc] around, join with a sl st into first st. (12 sc)

Rnd 7: [Sc2tog] around, join with a sl st into first st. (6 sc)

Fasten off yarn and sew up final hole to secure.

Abbreviations (see page 19)

ch chain

rep repeat

rnd round

sc single crochet

sc2tog single crochet 2 together

sl st slip stitch

Techniques (see pages 10–19)

Decreasing

Fastening off

Joining in a new color

Sewing on buttons

Starting to work in the round

② Make the features

Make a paper template for the ear and leg shapes, drawing them freehand. Cut out the template and pin it to the red felt and cut out two ears and four legs. Cut a thin, pointed strip for the tail.

3 Sew on the features

Using a sewing needle and matching thread, sew the ears to the side of the head using small stitches and hiding the end of the thread in the crochet. Do the same to sew on the legs, placing them on opposite sides at the top and bottom of the dog. Attach the tail so that it points up and is wagging!

4 Sew the eyes

Draw around something round, such as a cotton reel or button, or cut out two circles freehand for the eyes. Sew them to the face and then add two small buttons—you can give your dog a funny expression by sewing the pupils in different places.

5 Sew the nose and mouth

Cut a small triangle of red felt for the nose and sew it in place. Use a left-over piece of red yarn and a darning needle to sew the mouth using backstitch.

A striped sausage dog just for you!

Round striped pillow cover

Crochet is perfect for making circles and this pillow cover is a great beginner's project using a rainbow of lovely yarns that would look great in any bedroom.

You will need

1 x 1¾ oz (50 g) ball (98 yd/90 m)
Rowan Belle Organic Aran
(50% organic wool, 50% cotton) in
each of:

Yarn A: shade 209, Robin's Egg

Yarn B: shade 203, Orchid

Yarn C: shade 205, Rose

Yarn D: shade 212, Zinc

Yarn E: shade 206, Poppy

Yarn F: shade 211, Cilantro

H/8 (5 mm) crochet hook

Darning needle

16 in. (40 cm) round pillow form

Measurements

To fit a 16 in. (40 cm) diameter round
pillow form

Gauge

14dc by 8 rows over a 4 in.
(10 cm) square using H/8 (5 mm)
hook, or size required to obtain
correct gauge.

1 Crochet the cover (make 2 sides)

Using h/8 (5 mm) hook and yarn A, ch6, join into a ring with sl st into first ch.

Rnd 1: Ch3 (counts as first dc), 11dc into ring, join with a sl st into top of first 3-ch.
Change to yarn B.

Rnd 2: Ch3, 1dc in same st, 2dc in every st to end of round, join with a sl st into top of first 3-ch. (24 sts)
Change to yarn C.

Rnd 3: Ch3, 1dc in same st, *1dc in next st, 2dc in each of next 2 sts; rep from * to last 2 sts, 1dc in next st, 2dc in last st, join with a sl st into top of first 3-ch. (40 sts)
Change to yarn D.

Rnd 4: Ch3, 1dc in same st, *1dc in each of next 3 sts, 2dc in next st; rep from *to last 3 sts, 1dc in each of last 3 sts, join with a sl st into top of first 3-ch. (50 sts)
Change to yarn E.

Rnd 5: Ch3, 1dc in same st, *1dc in each of next 4 sts, 2dc in next st; rep from * to last

Abbreviations (see page 19)

ch chain

dc double crochet

sc single crochet

sl st slip stitch

st(s) stitches

Techniques (see pages 10–19)

Fastening off

Making fabric

Starting to work in the round

4 sts, 1dc in each of last 4 sts, join with sl st into top of first 3-ch. (60 sts)

Change to yarn F.

Rnd 6: Ch3, 1dc in same st, *1dc in each of next 5 sts, 2dc in next st; rcp from *to last 5 sts, 1dc in each of last 5 sts, join with a sl st into top of first 3-ch. (70 sts)

Change to yarn A.

Rnd 7: Ch3, 1dc in same st, *1dc in each of next 6 sts, 2dc in next st; rep from * to last 6 sts, 1dc in each of last 6 sts, join with a sl st into top of first 3-ch. (80 sts)

Change to yarn B.

Rnd 8: Ch3, 1dc in same st, *1dc in each of next 7 sts, 2dc in next st; rep from *to last 7 sts, 1dc in each of last 7 sts, join with a sl st into top of first 3-ch. (90 sts)

Change to yarn C.

Rnd 9: Ch3, 1dc in same st, *1dc in each of next 8 sts, 2dc in next st; rep from * to last 8 sts, 1dc in each of last 8 sts, join with a sl st into top of first 3-ch. (100 sts)

Change to yarn D.

Rnd 10: As Rnd 5. (120 sts)

Change to yarn E.

Rnd 11: Ch3, 1dc in same st, *1dc in each of next 11 dc, 2dc in next st; rep from * to last 11 dc, 1dc in each of last 11 dc, join with a sl st into top of first 3-ch. (130 sts)

Change to yarn F.

Rnd 12: Ch3, 1dc in same st, *1dc in each of next 12 dc, 2dc in next st; rep from * to last 12 dc, 1dc in each of last 12 dc, join with a sl st into top of first 3-ch.

Change to yarn A.

Rnd 13: As Rnd 7.

Change to yarn B.

Rnd 14: Ch3, 1dc in same st, *1dc in each of next 15 dc, 2dc in next st, rep from * to last 15 dc, 1dc in each of last 15 dc, join with a sl st into top of first 3-ch.

Change to yarn C.

Rnd 15: Ch3, 1dc in same st, *1dc in each of next 16 dc, 2dc in next st; rep from * to last 16 dc, 1dc in each of last 16 dc, join with a sl st into top of first 3-ch.

Change to yarn D.

Rnd 16: As Rnd 9.

Fasten off yarn.

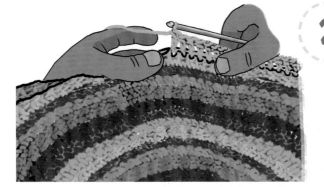

2 Sew together

Put the cover pieces together with wrong sides facing. Insert the hook into both sides and, using yarn A, make 1 ch. Make 1sc into each st, putting hook through both sides and joining sides together. Leave a big enough gap to push through the pillow form.

Insert the pillow form

(3) With the hook and yarn still attached, carefully insert the pillow form through the gap. Continue to crochet in sc until the seam is fully joined together.

Fasten off yarn. Weave in ends.

CHAPTER 4

Perfect Gifts

Baby bouncers

Little crochet balls for tiny hands—lovely for babies to hold, throw, or crawl after. These are great to practice crocheting in the round. The instructions are for making them in one color but you could make them striped if you feel like it.

You will need

Small amounts of each of (choose one color for a plain ball or combine them to make fun stripes):

King Cole Merino Blend DK (100% merino wool) in shade 55, gold and shade 787, fuchsia

Debbie Bliss Cashmerino DK (55% merino wool, 33% microfiber, 12% cashmere) in: shade 017, lilac and shade 029, light green

Rowan Belle Organic DK (50% organic wool, 50% cotton) in shade 014, robin's egg

Rooster Almerino DK (50% baby alpaca, 50% merino wool) in shade 203, strawberry cream

US 6 (4 mm) crochet hook

Stitch marker

Fiberfill stuffing

Measurements

2¾ in. (7 cm) diameter

Gauge

Exact gauge isn't important for this project.

1 Crochet the ball

Place a stitch marker at the beginning of each round.

Rnd 1: Ch2, 6sc in second ch from hook.

Rnd 2: 2sc in each st. (12 sts)

Rnd 3: *1sc in next st, 2sc; rep from * to end. (18 sts)

Rnd 4: *1sc in each of next 2 sts, 2sc; rep from * to end. (24 sts)

Rnd 5: *1sc in each of next 3 sts, 2sc; rep from * to end. (30 sts)

Rnds 6–10: 1sc in each st. (30 sts)

Rnd 11: *1sc in each of next 3 sts, sc2tog; rep from * to end. (24 sts)

Rnd 12: *1sc in each of next 2 sts, sc2tog; rep from * to end. (18 sts)

Rnd 13: *1sc in next st, sc2tog; rep from * to end. (12 sts)

Stuff the ball through the opening with small amounts of fiberfill, until it is well shaped and firm.

Rnd 14: Sc2tog around until hole closes.

Fasten off yarn.

Use the darning needle to sew in the ends.

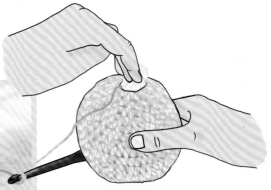

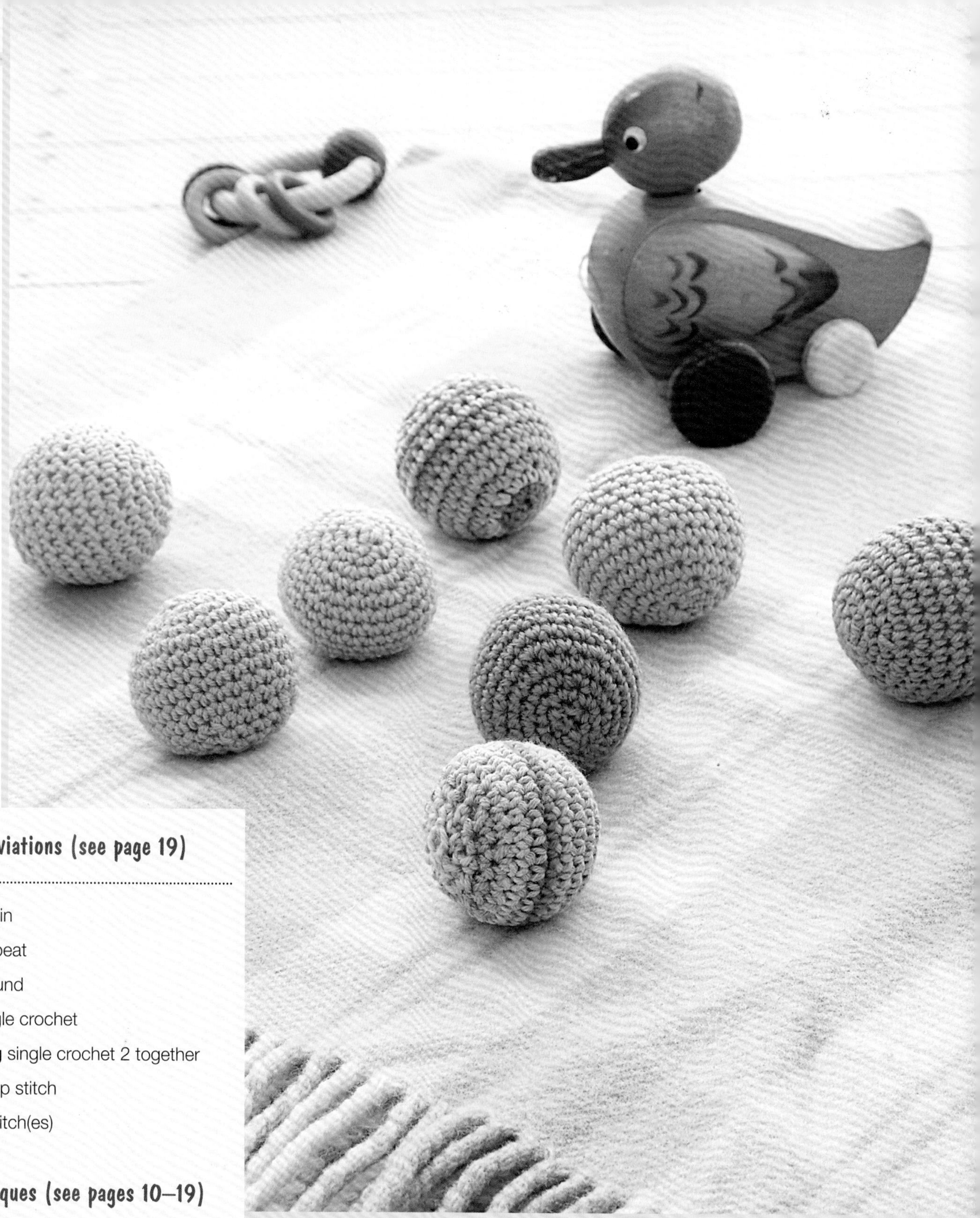

Abbreviations (see page 19)

ch chain

rep repeat

rnd round

sc single crochet

sc2tog single crochet 2 together

sl st slip stitch

st(s) stitch(es)

Techniques (see pages 10–19)

Decreasing

Fastening off

Marking rounds with a stitch marker

Starting to work in the round

Playtime for baby

Cheryl the snail

Cheryl makes a great addition to your cuddly toy collection. If you'd like to crochet her as a gift for a little baby or toddler, replace the safety eyes with pompoms or embroider eyes using a few stitches of black yarn.

You will need

1 x 1¾ oz (50 g) ball (124 yd/112 m) Rooster Almerino DK (50% baby alpaca, 50% merino wool) in each of:

Yarn A: shade 207, gooseberry

Yarn B: shade 203, strawberry cream

Small amount of Rowan Pure Wool DK (100% superwash wool), in Yarn C: shade 032, gilt

US 6 (4 mm) crochet hook

Pair of safety eyes

Fiberfill stuffing

Measurements

Approx. 5 in. (12.5 cm) tall

Gauge

Exact gauge isn't important for this project but make sure that you crochet tightly so that the stuffing does not show.

1. Crochet the head, body and tail (make all as one)

Begin at the tail end. Using US 6 (4 mm) hook and yarn A, ch2.

Row 1: 1sc in second ch from hook, turn.

Row 2: Ch1, 2sc in next st, turn.

Row 3: Ch1, 2sc in each st, turn. (4 sts)

Row 4: Ch1, 2sc in first st, 1sc in each of next 2 sts, 2sc in last st, turn. (6 sts)

Row 5: Ch1, 1sc in each of next 2 sts, 2sc in next st, 1sc in next 3 sts, sl st into first chain. (7 sts)

Rnd 1: 2sc in each st. (14 sts)

Rnds 2–9: 1sc in each st. (14 sts)

Rnds 10–11: 1sc in each of next 4 sts, sl st in next 6 sts, 1sc in next 4 sts.

Rnds 12–21: 1sc in each st. (14 sts)

Insert the eyes and secure them with a few stitches. Stuff the body firmly with small amounts of fiberfill stuffing, keeping the tail

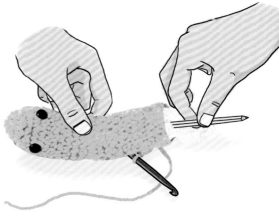

flat and the body in the upright position. Use the end of a pencil or the blunt end of a crochet hook to push the stuffing in well.

Rnd 22: 1sc in each of next 2 sts, sc2tog, 1sc in each of next 2 sts, sc2tog, 1sc in each of next 2 sts, sc2tog, 1sc in each of last 2 sts. (11 sts)

Rnd 23: 1sc in each of next 2 sts, sc2tog, 1sc in each of next 2 sts, sc2tog, 1sc in each of last 3 sts. (9 sts)

Rnd 24: Sc2tog, 4 times, 1sc in last sc. (5 sts)

Fasten off yarn.

Abbreviations (see page 19)

ch chain

hdc half double crochet

rep repeat

rnd(s) round(s)

sc single crochet

sc2tog single crochet 2 together

sl st slip stitch

st(s) stitch(es)

Techniques (see pages 10–19)

Fastening off

Sewing on buttons

Starting to work in the round

The cutest snail you'll meet!

(2) Crochet the shell

Using US 6 (4 mm) hook and yarn B, ch2.

Rnd 1: 6sc in second ch from hook.

Rnd 2: 2sc in each st. (12 sts)

Rnd 3: *1sc in next st, 2sc in next st; rep from * to end. (18 sts)

Rnd 4: *1sc in each of next 2 sts, 2sc in next st; rep from * to end. (24 sts)

Rnd 5: *1sc in each of next 3 sts, 2sc in next st; rep from * to end. (30 sts)

Rnds 6–8: 1sc in each st.

Rnd 9: 1sc in each of next 3 sts, sc2tog; rep from * to end. (24 sts)

Rnd 10: *1sc in each of next 2 sts, sc2tog; rep from * to end. (18 sts)

Rnd 11: 1sc in each st.

With the hook still attached, stuff the shell firmly with small amounts of fiberfill stuffing.

Rnd 12: *1sc in next st, sc2tog; rep from * to end. (12 sts)

Rnd 13: Sc2tog to end. (12 sts)

Rnd 14: Skip 1 st, 1sc in next st; rep from * to end.

Fasten off yarn.

Pin and sew the shell to the body by attaching the left side of the shell to the upper right side of the body, and the base of the shell to the top of the lower part of the body.

You could also try making a striped shell or just crochet the body and antennae to make a cuddly caterpillar!

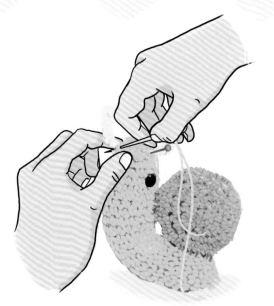

3 Crochet the antennae (make 2)

Using US 6 (4 mm) hook and yarn C, ch7, 2hdc in second ch from hook, sl st in each ch to end.

Fasten off yarn.

Pin and sew the antennae to either side of the head.

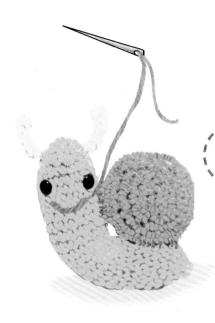

4 Add the mouth

Using yarn B, sew two curving straight stitches between the eyes for a sweet, smiling mouth.

Egg cozies

Keep your boiled eggs warm with these cute little cozies. Quick to make in the round and using bright yarn, they are perfect gifts or breakfast table treats. These are a great way to learn to crochet in the round. To make them even prettier you can add a different colored border, or to add beads follow the instructions in step 2.

You will need

1 x 1¾ oz (50 g) ball (131 yd/120 m) Rowan Belle Organic DK (50% organic wool, 50% cotton) in each of:

shade 012, tomato

shade 009, hibiscus

shade 014, robin's egg

shade 016, cilantro

1 x 1¾ oz (50 g) ball (124 yd/112 m) Rooster Almerino DK (50% baby alpaca, 50% merino wool) in shade 10, custard

E/4 (3.5 mm) crochet hook

Darning needle

Sewing needle and thread

2½ in. (6 cm) length x ½ in. (1.5 cm) wide ribbon for each cozy

15 beads (optional)

Measurements

6 in. (15.5 cm) circumference

Gauge

Exact gauge isn't important for this project.

1 Crochet the cozy (without beads)

Using E/4 (3.5 mm) hook and your chosen color, ch2, 6sc in second ch from hook.

Rnd 1: 2sc in each st to end. (12 sts)

Rnd 2: 2sc in each st to end. (24 sts)

Rnds 3–7: 1sc in each st.

Rnd 8: *1sc, sc2tog; rep from * to end. (16 sts)

If using a contrasting color for the border, fasten off here and rejoin new color into fastened-off st.

Rnd 9: 1sc in each st, sl st in last st.

Fasten off yarn.

Turn cozy right side out.

2 Crochet the cozy with beads

Thread 15 beads onto the yarn before starting the cozy by threading the yarn onto a needle and passing the needle through the beads.

Rep Rnds 1–8 of cozy pattern.

Beaded rnd

Work next rnd very loosely.

Rnd 9: Place bead to back of each st and make 1sc in each st, sl st into last st.

Fasten off yarn.

Turn cozy with beads on the outside.

Make pretty cozies for breakfast treats

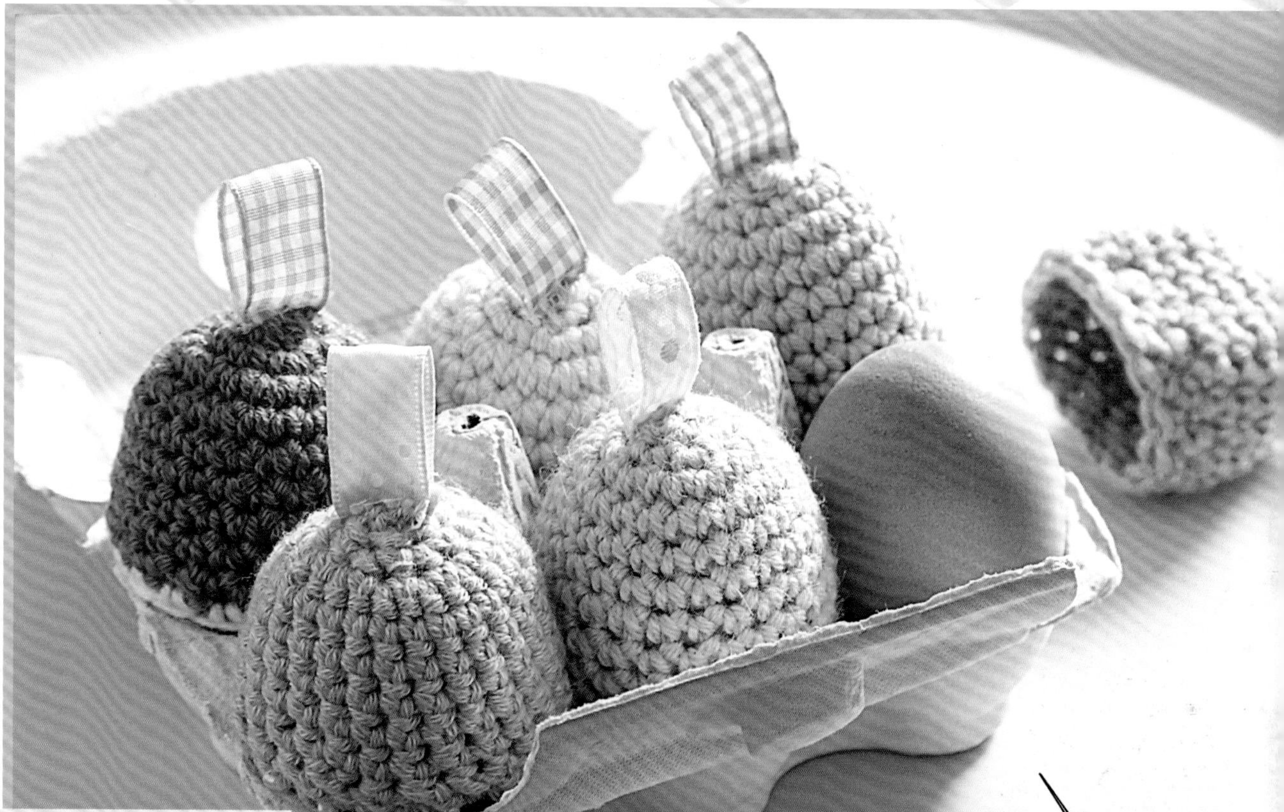

Abbreviations (see page 19)

ch chain

rep repeat

rnd round

sc single crochet

sc2tog single crochet 2 together

sl st slip stitch

st(s) stitch(es)

Techniques (see pages 10–19)

Fastening off

Joining in a new color

Starting to work in the round

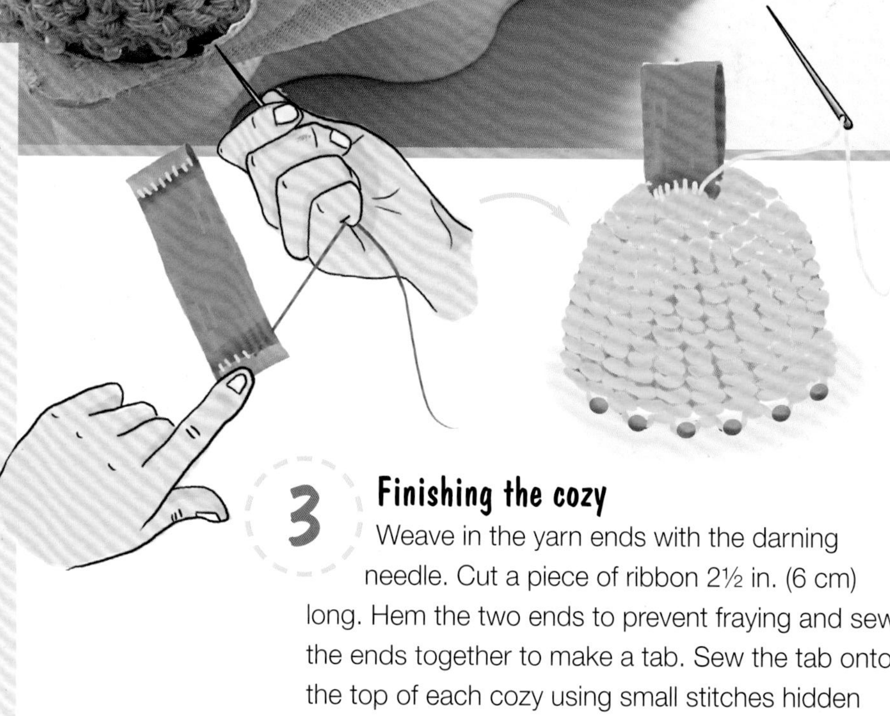

3 Finishing the cozy

Weave in the yarn ends with the darning needle. Cut a piece of ribbon 2½ in. (6 cm) long. Hem the two ends to prevent fraying and sew the ends together to make a tab. Sew the tab onto the top of each cozy using small stitches hidden inside the crochet.

Candy

This fun-to-make candy uses metallic and bright yarns to represent the shiny and colorful wrappers. Have fun and make your own candy store!

You will need

Yarn A: 1 x 3½ oz (100 g) ball (306 yd/280 m) DMC Petra no 3 (100% long staple cotton), in each of:

shade 5742, yellow

shade 53845, blue

shade 5907, green

shade 53805, pink

Yarn B: 1 x ¾ oz (20 g) ball (164 yd/150 m) DMC Metallic Crochet Thread (60% viscose, 40% metalized polyester), in each of:

shade L677, gold

shade L796, blue

D/3 (3.25 mm) crochet hook

Stitch marker

Darning needle

Fiberfill stuffing

Measurements

One size, each candy is approx. 4 in. (10 cm) long

Gauge

Exact gauge isn't important for this project but make sure that you crochet tightly so that the stuffing does not show.

① Crochet the candy

Using D/3 (3.25 mm) hook and any yarn A, ch20, join into a ring with a sl st into first ch.

Rnd 1: Ch1, 1sc in each st to end of rnd.

Rnd 2: 1sc in each st around.

Rep last row until candy measures approx. 3 in. (8 cm) long.

Fasten off yarn.

Join any yarn B to one open edge of candy.

Next rnd: Ch1, skip 1 sc, 5dc in next st, *skip 1 sc, 1sc in next st, skip 1 sc, 5dc in next st, rep from * to last st, skip last sc, sl st into first ch to join rnd.

Repeat the last round at the opposite end of the candy.

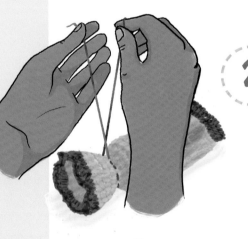

② Gather the end

Use a darning needle to weave in all ends. Use a needle to thread a piece of yarn in and out of the stitches all round one end of the candy, approx. 1 in. (2.5 cm) in from the end. Pull up the thread tightly to draw in the end of the candy wrapper and fasten off securely.

Make your own pick 'n' mix!

Abbreviations (see page 19)

ch chain

dc double crochet

rep repeat

rnd round

sc single crochet

Techniques (see pages 10–19)

Fastening off

Joining in a new color

Marking rounds with a stitch marker

Starting to work in the round

NOTE The candy is worked in a continuous spiral, do not turn throughout and do not join rounds.

3 Finish the candy

Stuff the candy with small tufts of fiberfill until it is nice and round. Use the end of a pencil or the blunt end of a crochet hook to push the stuffing in well. Sew round the opposite, open end of the candy in the same way as the first end, approx. 1 in. (2.5 cm) in from the end. Make lots of candy in different colors for a tempting treat!

Crochet cakes

These little cakes look so sweet you'll find it hard to believe you can't really eat them. You can make just one type or all three for a teatime treat for your dolls.

You will need

1 x 1¾ oz (50 g) ball (137 yd/125 m) Millamia Merino (100% merino wool), in each of:

Yarn A: shade 160, fawn

Yarn B: shade 122, petal

Yarn C: shade 104, claret

Yarn D: shade 124, snow

D/3 (3.25 mm) crochet hook

Stitch marker

Darning needle

Fiberfill stuffing

Sewing needle and thread

Beads and buttons for decoration

Measurements

Cupcake: approx. 4 in. (10 cm) diameter

Doughnut: approx. 4¾ in. (12 cm) diameter

Sponge cake: approx. 2½ in. (6 cm) diameter, 3½ in. (9 cm) tall

Gauge

Exact gauge isn't important for this project but make sure that you crochet tightly so that the stuffing does not show.

1 Crochet the cupcake

Using D/3 (3.25 mm) hook and yarn A, ch2.

Rnd 1: 6sc in first ch, join into a ring with a sl st.

Rnd 2: 2sc in each st around join with a sl st into top of first st. (12 sc)

Rnd 3: [1sc, 2sc in next st] around. (18 sc)

Rnd 4: [2sc, 2sc in next st] around. (24 sc)

Rnd 5: [3sc, 2sc in next st] around. (30 sc)

Rnd 6: [4sc, 2sc in next st] around. (36 sc)

Rnd 7: [5sc, 2sc in next st] around. (42 sc)

Rnd 8: [6sc, 2sc in next st] around, join with a sl st into top of first st. (48 sc)

Work 1 rnd even in sc (blo), join with a sl st into top of first st.

Work even in sc for 7 more rnds, in spirals, do not join rnds.

Next rnd: *Ch3, sl st (tfl) of next st; rep from * all round, join rnd with a sl st.

Fasten off yarn A.

Join yarn B to the unworked back loop in any st of last sc rnd.

Next rnd: 1sc (blo) in each unworked back loop of last sc rnd, join rnd with a sl st.

Work 4 rnds even in sc in spirals, do not join rounds.

Next rnd: [6sc, sc2tog] around, join rnd with a sl st. (42 sc)

Work 1 rnd even without shaping.

Next rnd: [5sc, sc2tog] around, join rnd with a sl st. (36 sc)

Work 1 rnd even without shaping.

Next rnd: [4sc, sc2tog] around, join rnd with a sl st. (30 sc)

Work 1 rnd even without shaping.

With the yarn and hook still attached, stuff the cake through the hole until it is firm and nicely shaped.

Next rnd: [3sc, sc2tog] around, join rnd with a sl st. (24 sc)

Next rnd: [2sc, sc2tog] around, join rnd with a sl st. (18 sc)

Next rnd: [1sc, sc2tog] around, join rnd with a sl st. (12 sc)

Next rnd: [Sc2tog] around, join rnd with a sl st. (6 sc)

Sew round the remaining hole and pull up to secure.

Abbreviations (see page 19)

blo back loop only

ch chain

rep repeat

rnd round

sc single crochet

sc2tog single crochet 2 together

tfl through front loop

Techniques (see pages 10–19)

Fastening off

Joining in a new color

Marking rounds with a stitch marker

Starting to work in the round

NOTE Pieces are worked in a continuous spiral, do not turn throughout and do not join rounds unless otherwise stated.

2 Add a cherry to the cupcake

Decorate the top of the cupcake with a large red button or glass bead for a cherry, if you like. Thread a beading or sewing needle with thread and knot the end. Bring the needle out in the position where you would like your bead, so that the knot is hidden inside the crochet. Thread a bead onto the needle and down the thread. Take the needle back in close to where it emerged, so that the bead sits on the cupcake. Take a few more stitches through the bead to secure it.

3 Crochet the sponge cake

Using D/3 (3.25 mm) hook and yarn B, ch2.
Rnd 1: 6sc in first ch.
Rnd 2: 2sc in each st around join with a sl st into top of first st. (12 sc)
Rnd 3: [1sc, 2sc in next st] around. (18 sc)
Rnd 4: [2sc, 2sc in next st] around. (24 sc)
Rnd 5: [3sc, 2sc in next st] around. (30 sc)
Rnd 6: [4sc, 2sc in next st] around. (36 sc)
Rnd 7: [5sc, 2sc in next st] around. (42 sc)
Rnd 8: [6sc, 2sc in next st] around. (48 sc)
Work 1 rnd even in sc (blo).
Work even in sc (blo) for 7 more rnds.

Change to yarn D and work even in sc (blo) for 2 more rnds.
Change to yarn C and work 1 rnd even in sc.
Change to yarn D and work even in sc (blo) for 2 more rnds.
Change to yarn B and work even in sc (blo) for 5 more rnds.
Next rnd: *6sc (blo), sc2tog (blo); rep from * around. (42 sc)
Begin to stuff cake to desired fullness.
Next rnd: [5sc, sc2tog] around. (36 sc)
Next rnd: [4sc, sc2tog] around. (30 sc)
Next rnd: [3sc, sc2tog] around. (24 sc)
Next rnd: [2sc, sc2tog] around. (18 sc)
Next rnd: [1sc, sc2tog] around. (12 sc)
Next rnd: [Sc2tog] around. (6 sc)
Fasten off yarn.
Sew round the remaining hole and pull up to secure.

4 Add sprinkles

Sew sprinkles on top of the cake either using a few single stitches of contrasting yarn or attach bugle beads, as for the cherry in step 2.

5 Crochet the doughnut

Using D/3 (3.25 mm) hook and yarn A, ch65, join into ring with a sl st into first ch, being careful not to twist the chain.
Rnd 1: Ch1, 1sc in each ch to end of rnd, join to first ch with a sl st.
Rnd 2: Ch1, 1sc (blo) in each st to end of rnd, join to first ch with a sl st.
Work last rnd 5 times more.
Change to yarn C.
Next rnd: Ch1, 1sc in each st to end of rnd, join to first ch with a sl st.
Work last rnd 9 times more.
Fasten off yarn leaving a long tail.

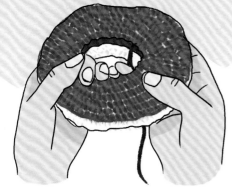

6 Sew together

Fold the top and bottom edges so that they meet and form a doughnut shape. Thread the yarn tail onto a darning needle and sew the edges together with whip stitch, without twisting, leaving a gap for stuffing.

Good enough to eat!

7 Finish the doughnut

Stuff the doughnut with fiberfill stuffing through the gap until it is firm and nicely shaped. Sew up the remaining seam. You can decorate the top of the doughnut with colorful bugle beads as in step 4, or sew sprinkles on top of the cake using a few single stitches of contrasting yarn.

Cafetière cozy

A fun and easy project that makes a great gift for coffee lovers. It will keep the coffee in the pot lovely and warm. The colors are changed at random as you work, for a multi-color effect.

You will need

1 x 1¾ oz (50 g) ball (103 yd/94 m) Rooster Almerino Aran (50% baby alpaca, 50% merino wool), in each of:

shade 305, custard

shade 310, rooster

shade 307, Brighton rock

shade 309, ocean

shade 302, sugared almond

shade 303, strawberry cream

shade 308, spiced plum

H/8 (5 mm) crochet hook

Darning needle

1 small button

Measurements

To fit a medium-size 4–6 cup cafetière, approx. 12 in. (31 cm) circumference

Gauge

16sc x 20 rows over 4 in. (10 cm) square, using H/8 (5 mm) hook or size to obtain correct gauge.

1 Crochet the cozy

Using H/8 (5 mm) hook and any color, ch46.

Row 1: 1sc in next ch from hook, 1sc in each ch to end, turn. (45 sts)

Row 2: Ch1, 1sc in each st to end, turn.

Rep Row 2, changing colors randomly every 2, 3 or 4 rows, until work measures 6¼ in. (16cm), or to just above handle of cafetière. Do not fasten off.

2 Make the buttonhole and button tab

Ch5, 1sc in next ch from hook, 1sc in each st to end.

Next row: 1sc in each st to last 4 sts, ch2, skip 2 sts, 1sc in each of next 2 sts.

Next row: Ch1, 1sc in each of next 2 sts, 2sc in next ch sp, 1sc in each st to end.

Next row: 1sc in each st to end. Do not fasten off.

Work sc around button tab by making 2sc around side, 1sc in each of the sts underneath to end. Make sl st into straight edge. Fasten off yarn.

3 Finish the cozy

With the wrong side facing you, join the two short edges by sewing them together for 1 in. (2.5 cm) up from the bottom, leaving the remainder open, using a matching yarn.

Abbreviations (see page 19)

ch chain

rep repeat

sc single crochet

sl st slip stitch

st(s) stitch(es)

Techniques (see pages 10–19)

Fastening off

Joining in a new color

Sewing on buttons

Turn

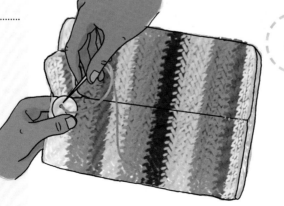

4 Sew the button

Turn right side out. Sew a button on the opposite side to the buttonhole tab to correspond with the buttonhole. Weave in the loose ends with a darning needle.

Keep the coffee steaming hot!

Jelly pot covers

These fun jelly pot covers are really quick and perfect for beginners. You can use any yarn—just choose two pretty colors for the perfect finish for a jar of homemade jelly. These would make great thank-you gifts for your teacher!

1 Crochet the cover
Both sizes

Using US 6 (4 mm) hook and yarn A, ch2, 6sc in second ch from hook, join into a ring with a sl st.

Rnd 1: Ch3 (counts as first dc), make 1dc in same st as 3ch, 2dc in next and each st to end, join with a sl st into top of first 3-ch. (12 sts)

Rnd 2: Ch3, make 1dc in same st as 3ch, 2dc in next and each st to end, join with a sl st into top of first 3-ch. (24 sts)

Rnd 3: Ch3, make 2dc in each of next 2 sts; *1dc in next st, 2dc in each of next 2 sts; rep from * to end, join with a sl st into top of first 3-ch. (40 sts)

Rnd 4: Ch3, make 1dc in each of next 2 sts, *2dc in next st, 1dc in each of next 3 sts; rep from * to last st, 2dc, join with a sl st into top of first 3-ch. (50 sts)

Rnd 5: Ch3, make 1dc in next st, *2dc in next st, 1dc in each of next 2 sts; rep from * to last st, 1dc, join with a sl st into top of first 3-ch. (66 sts)

For large size only

Rnd 6: Ch3, make 1dc in each st, join with a sl st into top of first 3-ch. (66 sts)

Fasten off yarn A and join yarn B.

Rnd 7: With the right side facing you, skip 1 st *5dc in next st, skip 1 st, sl st; rep from * to last st, sl st. Fasten off yarn.

You will need

Colorway 1 (light pink)

1 x 1¾ oz (50 g) ball (124 yd/112.5 m) Rooster Almerino DK (50% baby alpaca, 50% merino wool) in each of:

shade 203, strawberry cream (A)

shade 201, cornish (B)

Colorway 2 (lavender)

1 x 1¾ oz (50 g) ball (98 yd/90 m) Debbie Bliss Cashmerino Aran (55% merino wool, 33% microfiber, 12% cashmere) in shade 019, lilac (A)

1 x 1¾ oz (50 g) ball (124 yd/112.5 m) Rooster Almerino DK (50% baby alpaca, 50% merino wool) in shade 207, gooseberry (B)

Colorway 3 (green)

1 x 1¾ oz (50 g) ball (93 yd/85 m) Rowan Handknit Cotton DK (100% cotton) in shade 219, gooseberry (A)

1 x 1¾ oz (50 g) ball (124 yd/112.5 m) Rooster Almerino DK (50% baby alpaca, 50% merino wool) in shade 211, Brighton rock (B)

Colorway 4 (bright pink)

1 x 1¾ oz (50 g) ball (124 yd/112.5 m) Rooster Almerino DK (50% baby alpaca, 50% merino wool) in each of:

shade 211, Brighton rock (A)

shade 201, cornish (B)

US 6 (4 mm) crochet hook

Elastic band

Approx. 16 in. (40 cm) trimming or braiding in a contrasting color

Measurements

Standard: 6 in. (15 cm) diameter

Large: 7 in. (18 cm) diameter

Gauge

Exact gauge isn't important for this project.

You can use either double knit or Aran yarn—in Aran the cover will be slightly bigger.

2 Finish the cover

Place the cover on top of the jar lid and secure with an elastic band. Finish off by tying the trimming or braiding around the top, knotting to secure it in place.

Make pretty pots for a sweet treat

Abbreviations (see page 19)

ch chain

dc double crochet

rnd round

sc single crochet

sc2tog single crochet 2 together

sl st slip stitch

st(s) stitch(es)

Techniques (see pages 10–19)

Fastening off

Joining in a new color

Starting to work in the round

Mushroom

This fun mushroom is great for decorating your room and would look super cute on your bed sitting alongside Cheryl the snail on page 100 and the little penguin on page 122.

You will need

1 x 1¾ oz (50 g) ball (81 yd/75 m) Sirdar Click Chunky with wool (70% acrylic, 30% wool) in each of:

Yarn A: shade 142, lamb

Yarn B: shade 163, really red

H/8 (5 mm) crochet hook

Stitch marker

Darning needle

Fiberfill stuffing

Buttons for decoration

Sewing needle and thread

Scraps of yarn for embroidery

Measurements

Approx. 4 in. (10 cm) high

Gauge

Exact gauge isn't important for this project but make sure that you crochet tightly so that the stuffing does not show.

1 **Crochet the mushroom stalk**

Using H/8 (5 mm) hook and yarn A, ch2.

Rnd 1: 6sc in first ch made, do not join rnd.

Rnd 2: 2sc in each sc around. (12 sc)

Rnd 3: [2sc in next st, 1sc] around. (18 sc)

Rnd 4: [2sc in next st, 2sc] around. (24 sc)

Rnd 5: [2sc in next st, 3sc] around. (30 sc)

Work 1 rnd even in sc (blo), join with a sl st into top of first st.

Work even in sc for 5 more rnds, in spirals, do not join rnds.

Next rnd: [3sc, sc2tog] around. (24 sc)

Work 1 row even in sc.

Next rnd: [2sc, sc2tog] around. (18 sc)

Fasten off yarn A, join in yarn B.

Stuff the stalk before crocheting the cap.

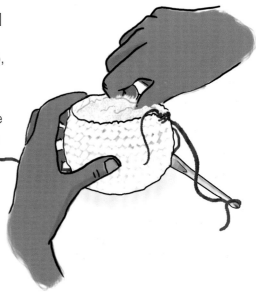

Cute as a button!

Abbreviations (see page 19)

blo back loop only

ch chain

rep repeat

rnd round

sc single crochet

sc2tog single crochet 2 together

sl st slip stitch

st(s) stitch(es)

Techniques (see pages 10–19)

Decreasing

Fastening off

Joining in a new color

Marking rounds with a stitch marker

Sewing on buttons

Starting to work in the round

NOTE The mushroom is worked in a continuous spiral, do not turn throughout and do not join rounds.

2 Crochet the mushroom cap

Work 1 row even in sc.

Next rnd: 2sc in each sc around. (36 sc)

Next rnd: [2sc in next st, 1sc] around. (54 sc)

Work 3 rows even in sc (blo).

Begin to decrease as follows:

Rnd 1: [4sc, sc2tog] around. (45 sc)

Work 1 row even in sc. Begin to stuff cap.

Rnd 3: [3sc, sc2tog] around. (36 sc)

Rnd 4: [2sc, sc2tog] around. (27 sc)

Rnd 5: [1sc, sc2tog] around. (18 sc)

Sc2tog around until hole closed. Fasten off yarn and stitch remaining hole closed.

3 Decorate the cap

Using a sewing needle and thread, sew a few buttons to the cap for spots.

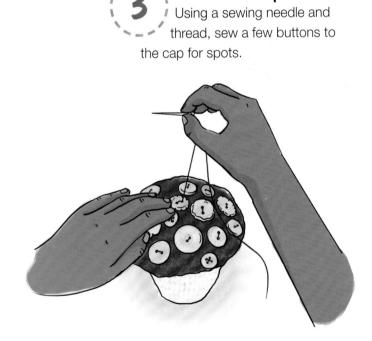

4 Add a face

Using a darning needle and some left-over yarn in a dark color, embroider a simple face on the stalk of the mushroom. Use a few straight stitches grouped together for the eyes, and add a smiley mouth in backstitch.

If you're making this as a gift for a baby, replace the buttons with circles of felt.

Juggling balls

Crocheted balls are fabulous for playing games such as Piggy in the Middle or Hacky Sack, and are perfect for learning to juggle. To give them some weight when juggling, fill with beans or PVC beanbag granules.

You will need

1 x 3½ oz (100 g) ball (437 yd/ 400 m) DMC Petra no 5 (100% long staple cotton), in each of:

Yarn A: shade 5742, yellow

Yarn B: shade 54230, blue

Yarn C: shade 5907, green

B/1 (2.25 mm) crochet hook

PVC beanbag beans

Darning needle

Measurements

One size, approx. 2½ in. (6 cm) diameter

Gauge

Exact gauge isn't important for this project, but make sure that you crochet tightly so that the beans do not show through the stitches.

1 Crochet the ball

Using B/1 (2.25 mm) crochet hook and any color yarn, ch2.

Rnd 1: 6sc in first ch made, join with a sl st into top of first st.

Rnd 2: Ch1, 2sc in each sc to end, join with a sl st into 1-ch. (12 sc)

Rnd 3: Ch1, [2sc in next st, 1sc] to end, join with a sl st into 1-ch. (18 sc)

Rnd 4: Ch1, [2sc in next st, 2sc] to end, join with a sl st into 1-ch. (24 sc)

Rnd 5: Ch1, [2sc in next st, 3sc] to end, join with a sl st into 1-ch. (30 sc)

Work 1 rnd even in sc without increasing.

Rnd 7: Ch1, [2sc in next st, 4sc] to end, join with a sl st into 1-ch. (36 sc)

Work 1 rnd even in sc without increasing.

Rnd 8: Ch1, [2sc in next st, 5sc] to end, join with a sl st into 1-ch. (42 sc)

Work 1 rnd even in sc without increasing.

Rnd 9: Ch1, [2sc in next st, 6sc] to end, join with a sl st into 1-ch. (48 sc)

Work 9 rnds even in sc without increasing.

Begin to decrease as follows:

Rnd 19: Ch1, [sc2tog, 6sc] to end, join with a sl st into 1-ch. (42 sc)

Work 1 rnd even in sc without decreasing.

Rnd 21: Ch1, [sc2tog, 5sc] to end, join with a sl st into 1-ch. (36 sc)

Work 1 rnd even in sc without decreasing.

Rnd 23: Ch1, [sc2tog, 4sc] to end, join with a sl st into 1-ch. (30 sc)

Work 1 rnd even in sc without decreasing. Begin stuffing the ball with beanbag beans through the hole until firm.

Rnd 25: Ch1, [sc2tog, 3sc] to end, join with a sl st into 1-ch. (24 sc)

Rnd 26: Ch1, [sc2tog, 2sc] to end, join with a sl st into 1-ch. (18 sc)

Rnd 27: Ch1, [sc2tog, 1sc] to end, join with a sl st into 1-ch. (12 sc)

Rnd 28: Sc2tog evenly all round. (6 sc)

Fasten off yarn.

Abbreviations (see page 19)

ch chain

rnd round

sc single crochet

sc2tog single crochet 2 together

sl st slip stitch

Techniques (see pages 10–19)

Decreasing

Fastening off

Joining in a new color

Making fabric

Starting to work in the round

NOTE The balls are worked in complete rounds.

Begin stuffing each ball from rnd 24 to ensure an evenly filled ball.

Work 2 rows of each color alternately, or in any order you like.

2 Finish the ball

Add some more beanbag beans through the hole in the top until the ball is nearly full, then thread the fastened-off yarn onto a darning needle and sew up the hole to close it.

How many balls can you juggle?

Penguin

This perky penguin is just calling to have his tummy squished! Why not try making him a scarf to keep him warm at the South Pole?

You will need

1 x 1¾ oz (50 g) ball (137 yd/125 m) Millamia Merino (100% merino wool), in each of:

Yarn A: shade 101, midnight navy

Yarn B: shade 142, daisy yellow

Yarn C: shade 124, snow white

D/3 (3.25 mm) crochet hook

Stitch marker

Darning needle

Fiberfill stuffing

Buttons for eyes

Sewing needle and thread

Measurements

One size, approx. 5½ in. (14 cm) tall

Gauge

Exact gauge isn't important for this project but make sure that you crochet tightly so that the stuffing does not show.

1 Crochet the head and body

Using D/3 (3.25 mm) crochet hook and yarn A, ch2.

Rnd 1: 7sc in first ch made, do not join rnd.

Rnd 2: 2sc in each sc around. (14 sc)

Rnd 3: [2sc in next st, 1sc] around. (21 sc)

Rnd 4: [2sc in next st, 2sc] around. (28 sc)

Rnd 5: [2sc in next st, 3sc] around. (35 sc)

Work 5 rnds even in sc without increasing.

Begin to decrease as follows:

Rnd 11: [Sc2tog, 3sc] around. (28 sc)

Rnd 12: [Sc2tog, 2sc] around. (21 sc)

Stuff head fully.

Work 2 rnds even in sc without decreasing.

Rnd 15: [2sc in next st, 2sc] around. (28 sc)

Rnd 16: [2sc in next st, 3sc] around. (35 sc)

Rnd 17: [2sc in next st, 4sc] around. (42 sc)

Work 1 rnd even in sc without increasing.

Rnd 19: [2sc in next st, 5sc] around. (49 sc)

Work 1 rnd even in sc without increasing.

Rnd 21: [2sc in next st, 6sc] around. (56 sc)

Work 1 rnd even in sc without increasing.

Rnd 22: [2sc in next st, 7sc] around. (63 sc)

Work 3 rnds even in sc without increasing.

Begin to decrease, as follows:

Rnd 26: [Sc2tog, 7sc] around. (56 sc)

Work 1 rnd even in sc without decreasing.

Rnd 28: [Sc2tog, 6sc] around. (49 sc)

Work 1 rnd even in sc without decreasing.

Rnd 30: [Sc2tog, 5sc] around. (42 sc)

Give your penguin a name

Work 1 rnd even in sc without decreasing. With the hook still attached, begin to stuff the body through the hole.

Rnd 32: [Sc2tog, 4sc] around. (35 sc)

Rnd 33: [Sc2tog, 3sc] around. (28 sc)

Rnd 34: [Sc2tog, 2sc] around. (21 sc)

Rnd 35: [Sc2tog, 1sc] around. (14 sc)

Rnd 36: [Sc2tog] around. (7 sc) Fasten off yarn and sew up the hole in the top of the head to secure.

Abbreviations (see page 19)

ch chain

dc double crochet

sc single crochet

sc2tog single crochet 2 together

rnd round

Techniques (see pages 10–19)

Fastening off

Sewing on buttons

Marking rounds with a stitch marker

Starting to work in the round

NOTE The wings and feet are worked in rows, turn at the end of each row.

The body and beak are worked in continuous spiral rounds, do not turn throughout and do not join rounds.

Crochet the feet (make two)

Using D/3 (3.25 mm) crochet hook and yarn B, ch4.

Row 1: 1sc in 2nd ch from hook, 1sc in each ch to end, turn. (3 sc)

Row 2: Ch1, 2sc in first st, 1sc, 2sc in last st, turn. (5 sc)

Row 3: Ch1, 1sc to end of row, turn.

Row 4: Ch1, 2sc in first st, 1sc, 2sc in last st, turn. (7 sc)

Row 5: Ch1, 1sc to end of row.

Fasten off yarn.

3 Crochet the wings (make two)

Using D/3 (3.25 mm) crochet hook and yarn A, ch3.

Row 1: 1sc in 2nd ch from hook, 1sc in next chain, turn. (2 sc)

Row 2: Ch1, 2sc in first st, 2sc in last st, turn. (4 sc)

Row 3: Ch1, 2sc in first st, 2sc, 2sc in last st, turn. (6 sc)

Rows 4–6: Ch1, 1sc to end of row, turn.

Fasten off yarn.

4 Crochet the beak

Using D/3 (3.25 mm) crochet hook and yarn B, ch3.

Work in the round in spirals.

Rnd 1: 5sc in 2nd ch from hook, do not turn.

Work 1 rnd even.

Rnd 3: 2sc in each sc around. (10 sc)

Fasten off yarn.

Crochet the tummy

Using D/3 (3.25 mm) crochet hook and yarn C, ch2.

Work in the round in spirals.

Rnd 1: 6sc in 2nd ch from hook, do not turn.

Rnd 2: 2sc in each sc around. (12 sc)

Rnd 3: [1sc, 2sc in next st] around. (18 sc)

Rnd 4: 3sc, 3dc, 6sc, 3dc, 1sc to end of rnd, join with a sl st to top of first sc. Fasten off yarn.

Sew on the wings and feet

Using a darning needle, sew the wings to the sides of the body and the feet to the bottom of the body. You can use the yarn end to attach the pieces with whip stitch.

Sew on the tummy and beak

Using a darning needle and whip stitch, sew the white oval to the penguin's tummy. Then sew the beak to the middle of the head.

Sew on the eyes

Finally, sew on buttons for the eyes, hiding the end of the thread in the crochet.

Suppliers and Resources

The yarns used in these projects should be available from your local yarn or craft store. If you can't find the correct yarn, then try the websites listed here.

YARN SUPPLIERS

Debbie Bliss
www.debbieblissonline.com

Coats Craft Rowan Yarns
www.coatscrafts.co.uk

Purl Soho
www.purlsoho.com

Yarn Forward
www.yarnforward.com

Fyberspates
www.fyberspates.co.uk

Rooster Yarns
www.laughinghens.com

Rooster & Fyberspates
Knitcellaneous
120 Acorn Street
Merlin,
OR 97532
www.knitcellaneous.com

Bluefaced Leicester
Wool2Dye4
6000-K Boonsboro Road
Coffee Crossing
Lynchburg
VA 24503
www.wool2dye4.com

Lets Knit
www.letsknit.com

Michaels
Stores nationwide
1-800-642-4235
www.michaels.com

Unicorn Books and Crafts
www.unicornbooks.com

WEBS
www.yarn.com

Yarn Market
www.yarnmarket.com

STOCKISTS

A.C. Moore
Stores nationwide
1-888-226-6673
www.acmoore.com

Crafts, etc.
Online store
1-800-888-0321
www.craftsetc.com

Hobby Lobby
Stores nationwide
www.hobbylobby.com

Jo-Ann Fabric and Craft Store
Stores nationwide
1-888-739-4120
www.joann.com

Knitting Fever
Stockists of Debbie Bliss, Noro, and Sirdar yarns
www.knittingfever.com

Knitting Garden
Stockists of Rowan yarns
www.theknittinggarden.com

Laughing Hens
Wool, patterns, knitting & crochet suppliers online
www.laughinghens.com

Index

Acknowledgments

Key: t = top, c = center, b = bottom, l = left, r = right

Project makers

Catherine Hirst: pp 58, 86

Claire Montgomerie: pp 22, 24, 26, 34, 36, 40, 42, 44, 48, 60, 62, 66, 68, 74, 82, 84, 90, 93, 106, 108, 116, 120, 122

Nicki Trench: pp 30, 52, 70, 78, 88, 98, 100, 104, 112, 114

Photography

Emma Mitchell: pp 2, 3l, 3r, 8t, 19, 31, 33, 53, 55, 56l, 56c, 58, 59, 71, 73, 76, 77l, 77c, 78, 79, 81, 87, 88, 89, 97l, 97c, 98, 99, 101, 112, 113, 115

Martin Norris: pp 3c, 4, 5t, 5b, 6, 7, 8b, 9, 12, 15, 17, 18, 20, 21, 23, 25, 27, 29, 35, 37, 39, 41, 43, 45, 47, 49, 50, 51, 56, 57r, 61, 63, 65, 67, 68, 69, 75, 77r, 83, 85, 91, 92, 93, 95, 96, 97r, 102, 103, 105, 107, 109, 110, 111, 117, 119, 121, 123, 124